ULTIMATE MODERN
QUILT BLOCK COLLECTION

113 Designs for Making
Beautiful and Stylish Quilts

Daisy Dodge

Landauer Publishing

I dedicate this book to my family and friends who have come to understand and support my visceral need to create and *keep climbing*. I know this can be a lot to take at times, but thank you all for your continued understanding, cheerleading, and love.

To my mom, who has been an inspiration to me throughout my life, in every way imaginable. Thank you for all you did to help with this project, including the numerous late-night brainstorming sessions. This book would not have been possible without you by my side.

Lastly, for my husband, Michael. Your patience, endless encouragement, and love allowed me to tackle and accomplish this goal. Your unwavering support made this journey possible. I love you, still-again.

Ultimate Modern Quilt Block Collection

Landauer Publishing, www.landauerpub.com, is an imprint of Fox Chapel Publishing Company, Inc.

Copyright © 2022 by Daisy Dodge and Fox Chapel Publishing Company, Inc., 903 Square Street, Mount Joy, PA 17552.

Project Team
Managing Editor: Gretchen Bacon
Acquisitions Editor: Amelia Johanson
Editor: Christa Oestreich
Designer: Wendy Reynolds
Photographer: All photography by John Nantes unless otherwise stated; illustrations and photos on pages 13–15 by Daisy Dodge
Indexer: Jean Bissell

ISBN 978-1-63981-003-1

Library of Congress Control Number: 2022943418

We are always looking for talented authors. To submit an idea, please send a brief inquiry to acquisitions@foxchapelpublishing.com.

Note to Professional Copy Services:
The publisher grants you permission to make up to six copies of any quilt patterns in this book for any customer who purchased this book and states the copies are for personal use.

Printed in China
25 24 23 22   2 4 6 8 10 9 7 5 3 1

This book has been published with the intent to provide accurate and authoritative information in regard to the subject matter within. While every precaution has been taken in the preparation of this book, the author and publisher expressly disclaim any responsibility for any errors, omissions, or adverse effects arising from the use or application of the information contained herein.

Contents

Introduction

Hello fellow quilting artists! I am delighted to share my modern blocks with all of you. On the following pages, I have supplied templates and patterns for 113 blocks with both paper pieced and traditional instructions. The four quilts represented in this book are made from those blocks and are supplied with easy-to-follow directions to duplicate directly, but I also encourage all quilt designers to personalize their creations. The quilt blocks can mix and match in any configuration to make each quilt truly unique.

The featured quilts all utilize solid fabrics, allowing the color and quilt blocks themselves to be the star. However, adding prints could be interesting as well, creating another option for interpretation and discovery. Push the limits of your own creativity; experiment, explore, and question design. Experimentation is a gift you give yourself; it sparks growth and is a necessary component of innovation. Dive in. Play with color. Mix up the blocks. Let this book serve as a roadmap on your creative journey as you explore and discover something fresh and modern.

I've had to work hard recently to stay inspired in my work, longing for innovation in my own creativity. I felt as though I had exhausted the go-to techniques in my art and quilting, and I was determined to try something different. One way to unlock my imagination is by exploring and absorbing others' art, past and present. History is a treasure trove of ideation, and I find it to be a reliable kick start to my personal brainstorming.

I curled up in my comfy chair one gloomy Saturday afternoon, held a fresh-brewed cup of coffee, embraced my computer, and rabbit-holed into one online search after another, revisiting some of my favorite paintings and moments in art history. Before too long, I found myself getting reacquainted with a design style with which I have always had a fascination: the Bauhaus movement. Wedged between the two World Wars, this art school was founded by Walter Gropius in Weimar, Germany, in 1919. On the heels of the ornamentally floral Art Nouveau period, the Bauhaus movement was grounded in an abstract, geometric style with little to no influence from any design predecessors. It was seen as a brand-new way of thinking, rooted in technology and architecture, and a focus on function over form in its minimalist approach. The Bauhaus encouraged experimentation by pushing the boundaries in the world of design and brought with it an energy of freedom and creativity that is still seen in modern designs today. In addition to the Bauhaus being attributed by many as the birthplace of graphic design, several groundbreaking artists are also accredited to this period, including Wassily Kandinsky, Paul Klee, and Josef Albers.

After paging through a visual archive of Bauhaus images and works, I had an idea. I started to look at the Bauhaus posters and paintings through a different lens and broke down the artworks and designs into shapes—into quilting blocks. Grabbing my pencil, I scribbled modern block designs, echoing the essence of Bauhaus design. One search after another led to continued sketches and block layouts. Before I knew it, I was rounding 50 different block designs, then 60, then surpassing 100. Hours had passed. My coffee was cold. But none of that mattered. I was on the cusp of something new, something potentially great, and nothing could restrain my excitement and need to *keep going*. So I did. I cut out all the 1" x 1" (2.5 x 2.5cm) doodles and arranged them on the floor one design after another, not realizing that I was creating the foundation of this book.

Happy Quilting!

Quilt Gallery

The blocks in this book are very versatile and can be manipulated into endless quilt designs, one masterpiece after another. The following pages feature some of the finished quilts by myself and others, utilizing the blocks in this book (and a few variations as well!)

NO WAY OUT

Designed & pieced by Daisy Dodge
Quilted by Angie Vertucci

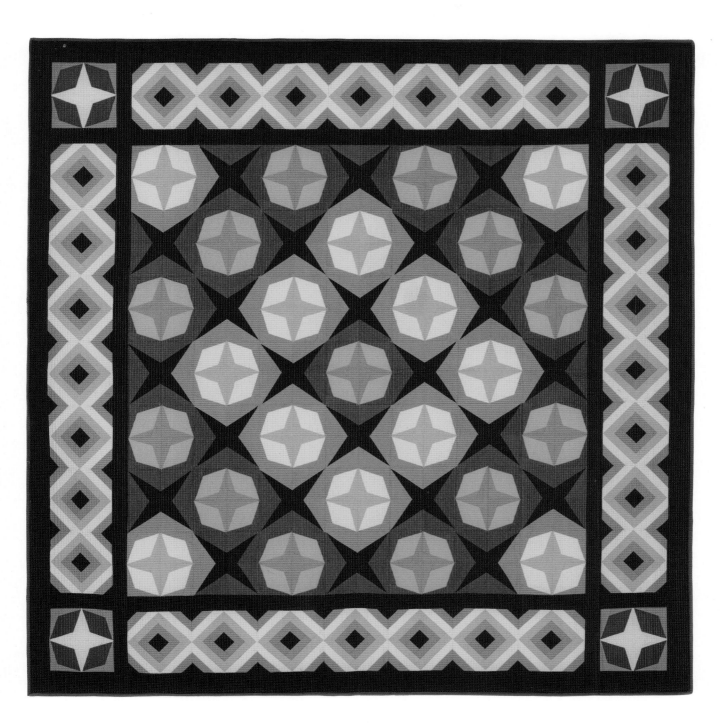

NEON NIGHTS

Designed & pieced by Daisy Dodge
Quilted by Angie Vertucci

ACID-WASHED JEANS

Designed & pieced by Diane Dodge
Quilted by Angie Vertucci

HARRY POTTER

Designed & pieced by Linda Franco
Quilted by Angie Vertucci

BERLIN

Designed & pieced by Daisy Dodge
Quilted by Angie Vertucci

THE BEAT GOES ON

Designed & pieced by Daisy Dodge
Quilted by Angie Vertucci

Paper Piecing Basics

This book has both traditional piecing patterns and foundation paper piecing directions. I prefer foundation paper piecing (FPP), and I have made dozens of quilts using the technique I have outlined in the directions below. There are variations to foundation paper piecing, so as you get more experienced with FPP, you may find shortcuts or preferences of your own.

FPP is a method of sewing fabric to paper to create intricate shapes in quilt block designs. It involves sewing the fabric directly to the paper templates, which then composes the final quilt block. Sometimes it takes many smaller blocks to be combined to make the desired final block. This is called a "complex block." But don't let the name scare you; it merely means there are multiple pieces needed to create the final block design.

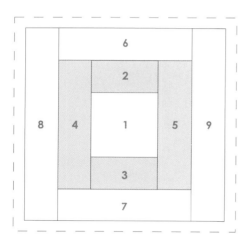

BASIC BLOCK

COMPLEX BLOCK

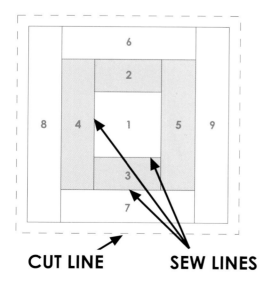

CUT LINE   **SEW LINES**

1. Photocopy the patterns in this book. Using the guide provided for each quilt, copy the block number indicated in the chart. Then cut the patterns out, leaving about ½"–¾" (1.2–1.9cm) of paper beyond the dashed line of the seam allowance. By eliminating the excess paper, it will be easier to work with the patterns when constructing your block. You will be sewing directly onto the paper patterns. The lines within the block are actual sewing lines, and the outer dashed line is the cut line, allowing ¼" (6.4mm) seam allowance. Set your machine stitch to smaller than usual. The smaller the stitch, the easier it will be to remove the paper later.

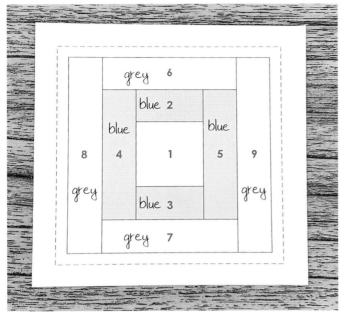

2. I find it helpful to write the fabric color for each piece directly on the paper. This will help keep the design integrity as you are assembling each block. Use a permanent marker or pencil for this step. I avoid ballpoint pens, as the ink may smear onto the fabric.

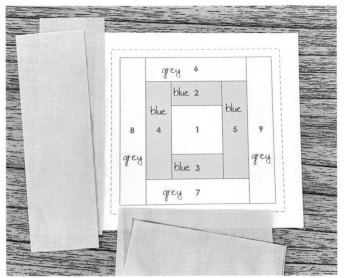

3. Before you begin piecing, cut your pieces. The beauty of FPP is there is no need to do any precise measuring or cutting. Sometimes I don't even use a ruler but rather cut freeform. Measurements are approximations, allowing you to move quite swiftly through the cutting process. I cut my pieces ½" (1.2cm) larger than the numbered shape. You can lay lighter fabrics directly onto the pattern and trace the shape using an erasable pen (I use FriXion) so it erases when ironed, or you can eyeball the cut to ensure the shape is larger than your desired shape. You can also utilize a lightbox to draw your shapes onto the fabric.

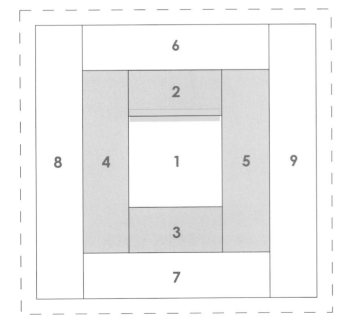

4. Once you have all the pieces cut for a block, begin to sew it together. The numbers on the block design indicate the order you will piece the block. Find numbers 1 and 2 on your pattern. The line between those two shapes (highlighted yellow) will be your first seam.

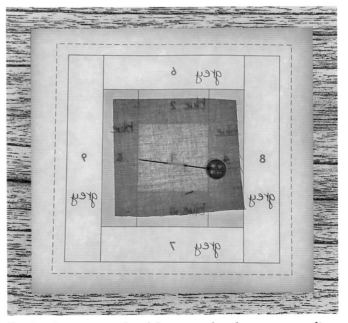

5. On the wrong side of the paper, lay the corresponding piece of fabric over the first shape. You may want to use a lightbox, or you can simply hold the paper and fabric up to a window or light source to ensure that the fabric extends beyond the lines of shape one. Pin this piece in place. **Note:** A water-soluble glue stick will also work.

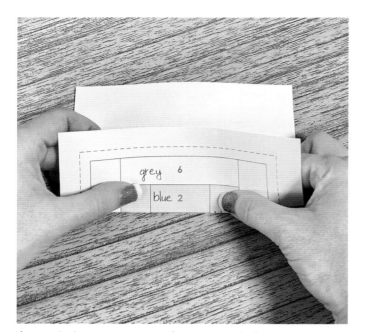

6. With the pattern paper face up, gently fold the paper back to create a crease along the line between pieces 1 and 2. This line will serve as a guide when placing your next fabric piece. Open the paper back up so the pattern is flat again.

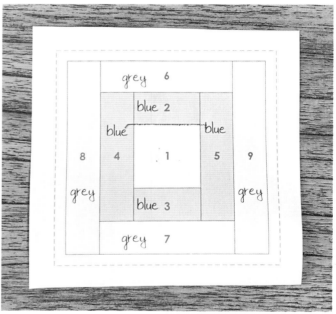

7. Overlap fabric piece 2 over piece 1, right sides of the fabric together. Ensure piece 2 aligns with the placement of piece 1 and overlaps your folded crease by at least ¼" (6.4mm). Pin this in place as well.

8. Turn the pattern over so the sewing lines are facing up and sew the line between shapes 1 and 2. Sew a couple stitches both before and beyond the sewing line. Trim your threads. This will ensure loose threads don't get tangled when assembling later pieces. **Note:** I am using a red thread to illustrate the stitching. A matching thread should be used for your projects.

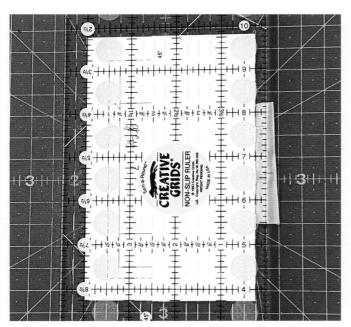
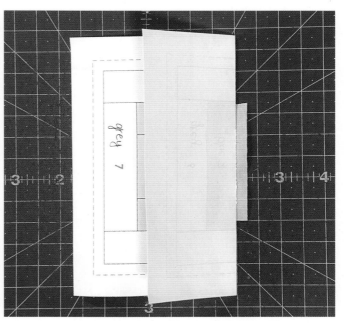

9. Remove the pins. With the pattern facing up, refold the paper only on the line between shapes 1 and 2. Align your ruler along the crease with ¼" (6.4mm) extending onto the fabric. Trim. Open your pattern back up and press your seam with a dry, hot iron. You now have a perfect ¼" (6.4mm) seam. Iron piece 2 open. Your first two pieces are complete.

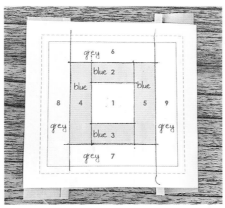
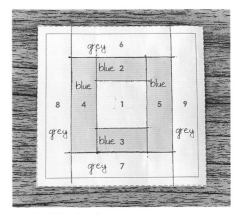

10. Repeat this process until all pieces of your block are attached. Once joined, give the block a heavy pressing to make it very flat. With paper side up, trim the block on the dashed cut line. It should be 5" (12.7cm). This will yield a 4½" (11.4cm) block when assembled.

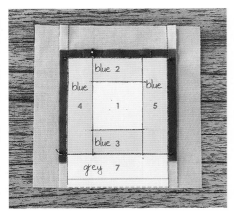
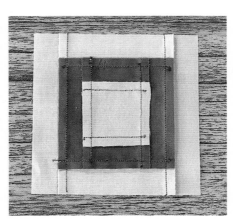

11. Starting with the outermost shapes first, begin gently tearing off your paper pieces one by one to finally reveal your finished block. Congratulations! Your first block is complete. You are now ready to dive into your first project!

Color Theory

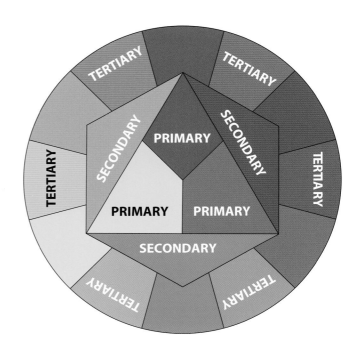

I find that one of the most exciting parts of the quilting process is choosing the color combination. The color palette of a quilt sets the tone and mood, and thereby is a key driver in conveying the intended emotion to a viewer.

When playing with color for my work, I like to utilize unexpected color combinations or employ a "zinger" color. The zinger is the color that is more different than the others and can act as a roadmap for the eye to follow when viewing the final piece.

The color wheels below show some solid basics to try when choosing your color combinations. Use these as a starting point and build from there. For added interest, try adding white or shades of gray; this can add a new dimension to the final quilt design. The possibilities are endless!

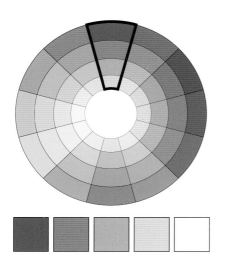

MONOCHROMATIC

The simplest use of color is the monochromatic approach. Although it might not be complicated, it is always effective. This is a good spot to add white or gray to play with color a bit against the core hue.

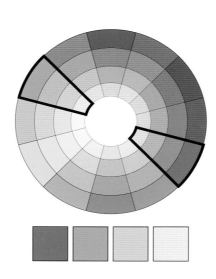

COMPLEMENTARY

These colors are directly across from one another on the color wheel. This choice is more exciting when you utilize the tints and shades within those two colors. Another way to approach complementary colors is to use many tints of one color and then only use one zinger tint of the other.

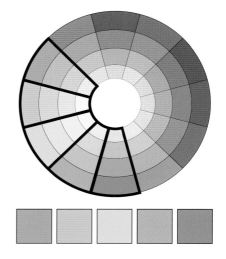

ANALOGOUS

Analogous color schemes include a main color and the colors on either side of that main color. You can also include two colors from either side of the main color. Depending on how this technique is used and which colors are selected, this approach can create a color "family" where all colors are related; by shifting a bit in either direction, a zinger can also become part of the color combo.

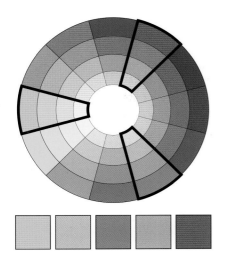

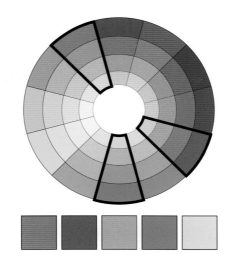

TRIAD

Simply put, it's an equilateral triangle: three colors equidistant from each other on the color wheel. This is one of my favorites. I find a natural energy forms when pulling together triads of color, which I find quite successful in my quilts. Adding grays or neutrals brings an added dimension to each of the colors.

SPLIT-COMPLEMENTARY TRIAD

This structure is still a triad, but in the shape of an isosceles triangle. This means the colors are not equidistant from each other. This slight twist on the triad approach brings a different depth to the color range.

Using Neutrals

In addition to grays complementing each color palette, neutrals, blacks, and whites are also fun to explore. Note how the same colors appear to change based on the additive color. Any way you slice it, these techniques are a launchpad to your imagination. I hope they help in kicking off your next masterpiece!

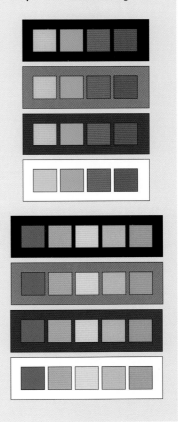

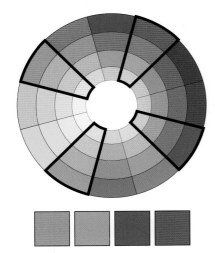

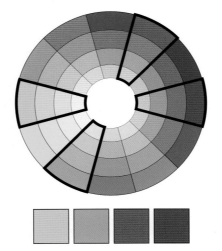

QUAD & RECTANGLE

These both utilize four colors: either a square with four equidistant colors or a rectangle with four colors that are not equidistant. Quads and rectangles are a good place to start when your goal is to create a very colorful quilt; they have a broad range of colors and act as a good alternate to a rainbow. Mathematically and flawlessly, quads and rectangles create more sophisticated color blends.

THE QUILTS

These next four projects use a variety of block designs, ranging in complexity of palette and layout. There are a variety of blocks in Valentino Francine and Bauhaus Sampler, contrasted with the simplicity of Racing Hearts. These projects highlight the versatility of the block designs. Treasure Island, a more advanced design approach, takes bold steps in utilizing more than two colors in each block, allowing secondary patterns to be formed within the design. The possibilities are truly endless and await your discovery and adaptation.

You may want to emulate the color placement of these quilts, use them as a starting point with your own twist, or depart from the colors and placement entirely. The choice is yours as you embark upon your journey and build your personal, one-of-a-kind creation!

Note: The patterns may also be enlarged or reduced as well. If doing so, remember to adjust your fabric requirements and outer seam allowance when trimming your final blocks. These blocks look just as lovely at 6" (15.2cm) and could be enlarged even more for bed quilts.

Bauhaus Sampler

This sampler quilt utilizes 91 unique block patterns and features sashing to offset the blocks. It's a delight to make as each block is its own work of art. Color placement is very important to maintain the "blended" look of this quilt design. All blocks are comprised of 2 colors. When creating your color scheme, start from the center. Decide colors A and B (in this case, aqua and teal). The next concentric round of blocks will require either color A or B. Here, aqua was the constant with ivory as the secondary color. Continue in this manner to complete your color plan. The Bauhaus Sampler will quickly become a favorite for generations to enjoy.

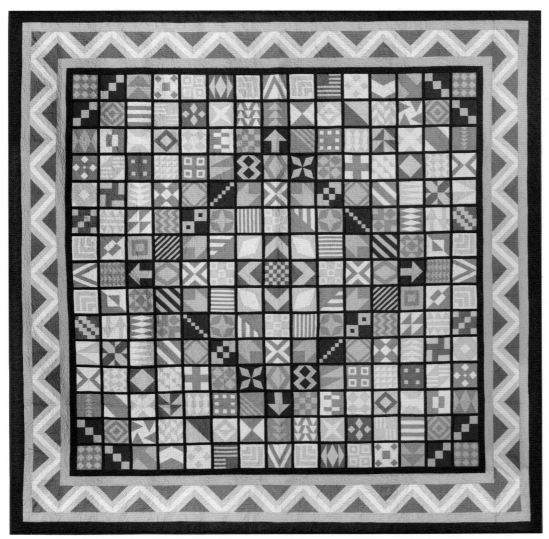

Designed & pieced by Daisy Dodge • Quilted by Angie Vertucci
Quilt size: 98½" x 98½" (250.2 x 250.2cm)

Materials
- Ivory fabric: 4½ yards
- Gray fabric: 2¾ yards
- Aqua fabric: 3½ yards
- Teal fabric: 2½ yards
- Lilac fabric: 2½ yards
- Purple fabric: ¾ yard
- Chocolate fabric: 2⅜ yards
- Backing: 11½ yards
- Batting: 11½ yards
- Binding: ⅝ yard

Note: Yardage requirements are approximate, as these may vary depending on personal cutting/assembly technique.

Quilt Body Assembly

1. The first step is to make the 225 blocks for the body of the quilt and the 68 blocks for the zigzag border. I recommend making all of these before you begin any quilt assembly. Using the charts on pages 24–26 and following Paper Piecing Basics on pages 12–15, piece the indicated number of blocks in each color combination:

    Color Combo 1: Ivory & Gray . . . . . . 56 blocks

    Color Combo 2: Aqua & Ivory . . . . . . 56 blocks

    Color Combo 3: Teal & Aqua . . . . 29 blocks

    Color Combo 4: Lilac & Purple . . . . . 28 blocks

    Color Combo 5: Gray & Lilac . . . . 56 blocks

    Border Blocks: Ivory, Aqua, & Teal . . 68 blocks

2. Once finished, separate them into stacks by color. This will make it easier to find each desired block for assembly.

3. Next, cut the sashing from the background fabric as follows:

    Chocolate: 1" x 5" (2.5 x 12.7cm) . . . . cut 210

    Chocolate: 1" x 75" (2.5 x 190.5cm) . . cut 14

4. Assemble the quilt body. Using the quilt roadmap on page 23, arrange the blocks into 15 stacks, one for each of the 15 rows of the quilt. Ensure all the blocks are piled facing the right direction based on the finished quilt diagram.

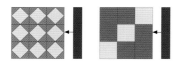

5. Attach one 1" x 5" (3 x 12.7cm) piece of sashing to the right side of each block, excluding the last block in each row. Press each seam allowance flat away from the block. Continue until the first 14 blocks in all 15 rows are complete. Before assembling the rows any further, I recommend double-checking that the blocks are oriented in the right direction. It will be much easier to correct any mistakes now versus later in the assembly process.

6. Ensure the blocks are arranged in sequential order from left to right. Begin sewing the blocks together, creating long assembled rows of 15 blocks each. Continue this process until all 15 rows of 15 blocks are complete.

7. For rows 1–14, attach the 1" x 75" (2.5 x 190.5cm) sashing pieces to the bottom of each row. There will be no sashing on the bottom of row 15. Press sashing flat.

8. To complete the quilt body, attach all rows together according to the diagram on page 21. Make sure the rows are being assembled in the correct order. The final design will only go together one way.

Adding the Borders & Finishing the Quilt

This quilt has five concentric borders, one of which is pieced from 68 border blocks (Block 91).

1. Cut the border pieces as follows:

    Border 1: Chocolate
    a) 1¾" x 75" (4.4 x 190.5cm) . . . . cut 2
    b) 1¾" x 77½" (4.4 x 196.9cm) . . . . cut 2

    Border 2: Lilac
    c) 2" x 77½" (5.1 x 196.9cm) . . . . cut 2
    d) 2" x 80½" (5.1 x 204.5cm) . . . . cut 2

    Border 3: Assembled zigzag
    Block 91 . . . . assemble 68
    e) 16 connected blocks:
       80½" (204.5cm) wide . . . . sew 2 sets
    f) 18 connected blocks:
       90½" (229.9cm) wide . . . . sew 2 sets

    Border 4: Lilac
    g) 2" x 90½" (5.1 x 229.9cm)   cut 2
    h) 2" x 93½" (5.1 x 237.5cm)   cut 2

    Border 5: Chocolate
    i) 3" x 93½" (7.6 x 237.5cm)   cut 2
    j) 3" x 98½" (7.6 x 250.2cm)   cut 2

    Binding: Purple
    2¼" x 42" (5.7 x 106.7cm)   cut 10

2. Utilizing the diagram on page 22, begin attaching borders. The numbers correspond to the order in which you should attach each piece. Always rotate in the same direction: top border, bottom border, left border, then right border. Attach borders 1–5 in this manner until finished.

3. Although the multiple borders may seem tedious, they are what bring the quilt blocks together and frame the final piece of art that is the quilt itself. The zigzag border in particular is key to giving this optical flair. To minimize trips to the ironing board, I sew two borders at a time before pressing. Sew top and bottom, then press; sew left and right, then press.

4. Layer the backing, batting, and quilt top. Baste, then quilt as desired.

5. Using the 2¼" (5.7cm)–wide strips, make and attach the binding to complete your masterpiece.

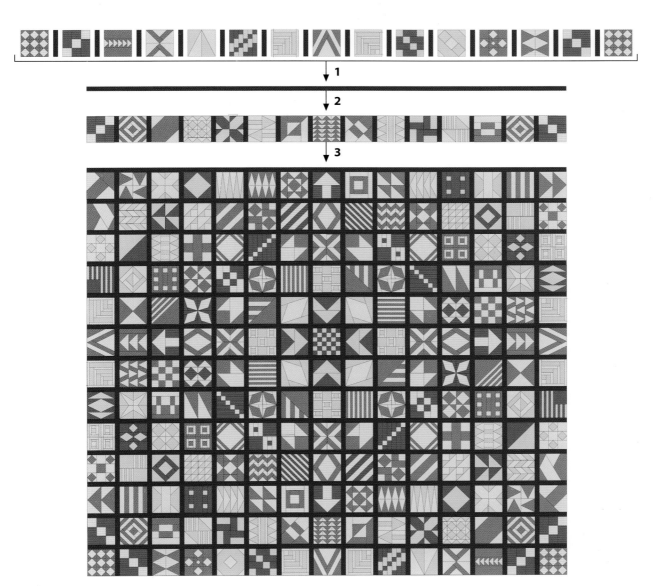

Quilt Body Assembly

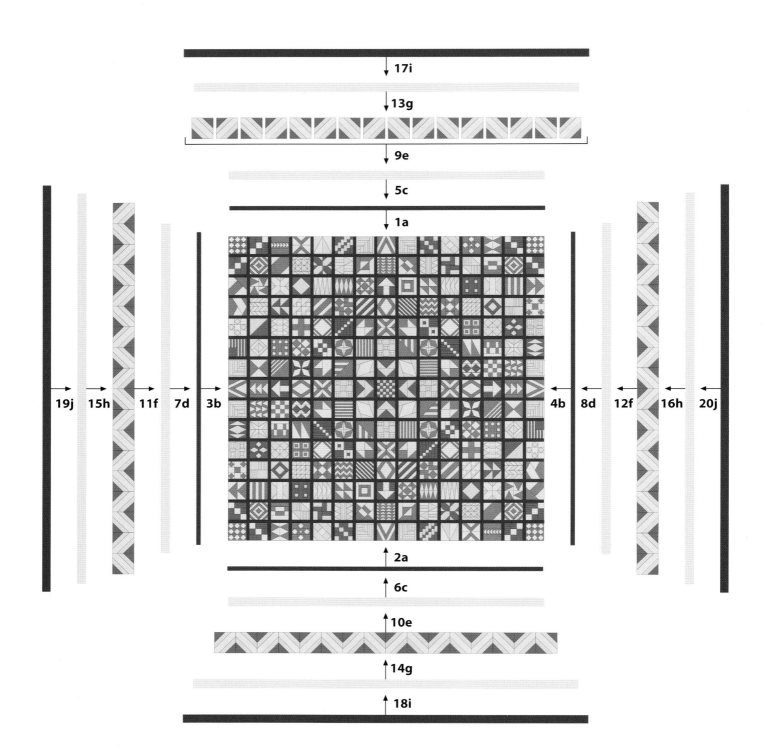

Finishing the Quilt

Quilt Roadmap

Use this roadmap to facilitate block placement and quilt layout.
Numbers correspond to the block patterns presented in this book.

91	91	91	91	91	91	91	91	91	91	91	91	91	91	91	91	91
91	77	62	75	15	38	59	45	8	45	53	37	4	85	62	77	91
91	62	88	22	39	60	32	16	79	14	29	52	36	3	88	62	91
91	74	23	40	61	41	17	82	63	80	13	28	51	35	2	86	91
91	24	46	57	42	18	71	67	78	70	81	12	27	50	34	1	91
91	47	55	43	19	72	68	90	5	90	69	72	11	26	49	33	91
91	56	44	20	73	65	83	6	30	7	83	68	84	10	25	48	91
91	45	21	87	66	90	7	31	58	31	6	90	64	89	9	45	91
91	8	77	63	78	5	30	58	54	58	30	5	78	63	77	8	91
91	45	9	89	64	90	6	31	58	31	7	90	66	87	21	45	91
91	48	25	10	84	68	83	7	30	6	83	65	73	20	44	56	91
91	33	49	26	11	72	69	90	5	90	68	72	19	43	55	47	91
91	1	34	50	27	12	81	70	78	67	71	18	42	57	46	24	91
91	86	2	35	51	28	13	80	63	82	17	41	61	40	23	74	91
91	62	88	3	36	52	29	14	79	16	32	60	39	22	88	62	91
91	77	62	85	4	37	53	45	8	45	59	38	15	75	62	77	91
91	91	91	91	91	91	91	91	91	91	91	91	91	91	91	91	91

Color Combo 1

Using the following charts, make the required number
of each block in the color family as indicated.

Block #		Quantity	Block #		Quantity	Block #		Quantity
1		x 2	9		x 2	17		x 2
2		x 2	10		x 2	18		x 2
3		x 2	11		x 2	19		x 2
4		x 2	12		x 2	20		x 2
5		x 4	13		x 2	21		x 2
6		x 4	14		x 2	22		x 2
7		x 4	15		x 2	23		x 2
8		x 4	16		x 2	24		x 2

Color Combo 2

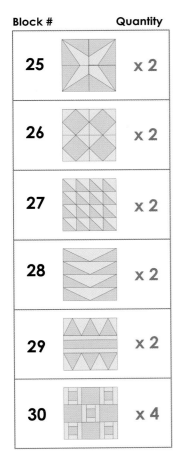

Block #		Quantity
25		x 2
26		x 2
27		x 2
28		x 2
29		x 2
30		x 4

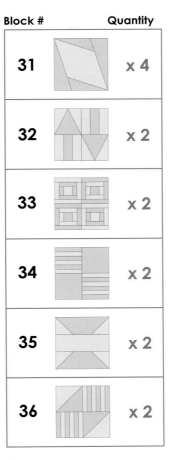

Block #		Quantity
31		x 4
32		x 2
33		x 2
34		x 2
35		x 2
36		x 2

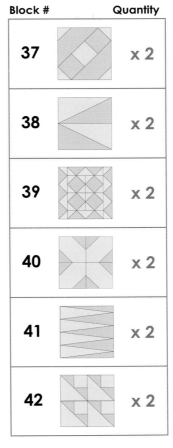

Block #		Quantity
37		x 2
38		x 2
39		x 2
40		x 2
41		x 2
42		x 2

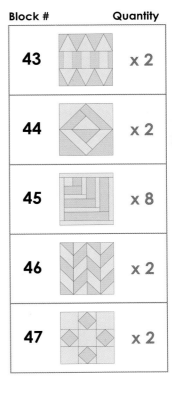

Block #		Quantity
43		x 2
44		x 2
45		x 8
46		x 2
47		x 2

Color Combo 3

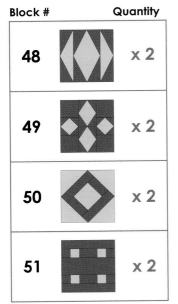

Block #		Quantity
48		x 2
49		x 2
50		x 2
51		x 2

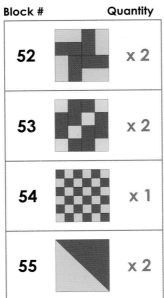

Block #		Quantity
52		x 2
53		x 2
54		x 1
55		x 2

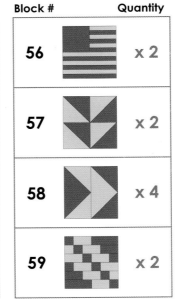

Block #		Quantity
56		x 2
57		x 2
58		x 4
59		x 2

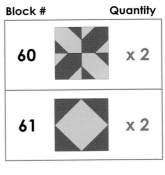

Block #		Quantity
60		x 2
61		x 2

Color Combo 4

Block #		Quantity	Block #		Quantity	Block #		Quantity
62	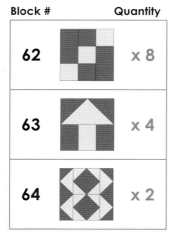	x 8	65	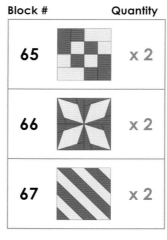	x 2	68		x 4
63		x 4	66		x 2	69		x 2
64		x 2	67		x 2	70		x 2

Color Combo 5

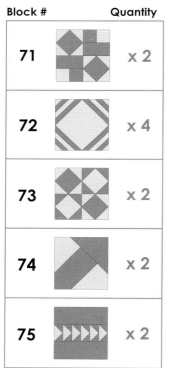
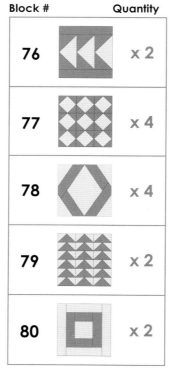
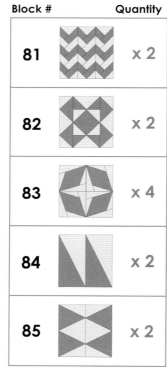
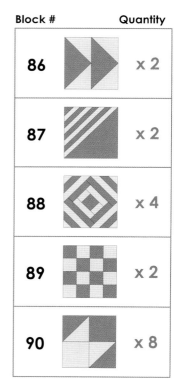

Block #		Quantity	Block #		Quantity	Block #		Quantity	Block #		Quantity
71		x 2	76		x 2	81		x 2	86		x 2
72		x 4	77		x 4	82		x 2	87		x 2
73		x 2	78		x 4	83		x 4	88		x 4
74		x 2	79		x 2	84		x 2	89		x 2
75		x 2	80		x 2	85		x 2	90		x 8

Border Blocks

Block #		Quantity
91		x 68

Bauhaus Sampler Color Variations

These color variations show how the personality of the quilt can change just by altering the palette. In all the examples, the sashing is the darkest color in the quilt to highlight each block design. Have fun playing with your color scheme to create your own unique combination!

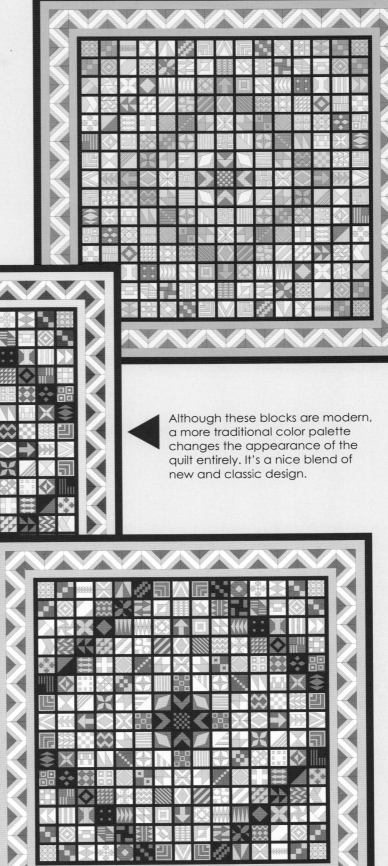

Although these blocks are modern, a more traditional color palette changes the appearance of the quilt entirely. It's a nice blend of new and classic design.

This design highlights the effect of a more controlled palette. Again, another successful interpretation of the Bauhaus Sampler design.

Racing Hearts

Racing Hearts is a bold and graphic quilt which utilizes only five block designs. Truly capturing the modern spirit, it exemplifies how beautiful simplicity can be.

Designed & pieced by Daisy Dodge • Quilted by Angie Vertucci
Quilt size: 36" x 36" (91.4 x 91.4cm)

Materials
- Gray fabric: 1¼ yards
- Ivory fabric: 1¼ yards
- Orange fabric: ¼ yard
- Yellow fabric: ¼ yard
- Pink fabric ¼ yard
- Backing: 2½ yards
- Batting: 2½ yards
- Border fabric (optional):
  Inner border fabric: ¼ yard
  Outer border fabric: ⅝ yard
- Binding: ⅜ yard

Note: Yardage requirements are approximate, as these may vary depending on personal cutting/assembly technique.

Quilt Body Assembly

1. Using the chart on page 30 and following Paper Piecing Basics on pages 12–15, piece the indicated number of half-square triangle blocks in each color combination:

Color Combo 1: Gray & Ivory . . . . . . 18 blocks

Color Combo 2: Gray & Orange . . . . 12 blocks

Color Combo 3: Gray & Yellow . . . . . 12 blocks

Color Combo 4: Gray & Pink . . . . 8 blocks

2. Once those are finished, separate them into stacks by color. This will make it easier to find each desired block for assembly.

3. Piece the nine graphic checks and stripes blocks as indicated.

Checks and Stripes: Gray & Ivory . . . . .9 blocks

4. Now cut the solid blocks and binding:

Pink Blocks: 5" x 5" (12.7 x 12.7cm). . . . . .cut 5

Ivory Binding: 2¼" x 42" (5.7 x 106.7cm) . . . . .cut 4

5. Using the roadmap on page 30, assemble the blocks in the quilt body as indicated.

Finishing the Quilt

Although this quilt has no borders, you may choose to add one or more to your liking. See example on page 31.

1. Layer the backing, batting, and quilt top. Baste, then quilt as desired.

2. Using the 2¼" (5.7cm)–wide strips, make and attach the binding to complete your quilt.

Color Combos

Using the chart below, make the required number of each block in the color family as indicated. **Note:** there is no block number for the solid pink squares. Follow the cutting directions on page 29, step 4.

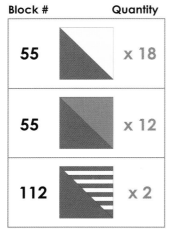

Block #		Quantity
55		x 18
55		x 12
112		x 2

Block #		Quantity
55		x 12
54		x 3
87		x 1

Block #		Quantity
55		x 8
67		x 3
x		x 5

Quilt Roadmap

Use this roadmap to facilitate block placement and quilt layout. Numbers correspond to the block patterns presented in this book.

55	55	55	55	67	X	55	55
54	55	55	55	55	55	55	55
55	55	87	55	55	55	54	55
55	55	X	55	67	55	55	X
55	55	55	55	55	55	55	112
55	55	55	54	55	55	55	55
X	67	55	55	55	55	55	55
55	55	55	55	55	112	X	55

Racing Hearts Color Variations

Although this quilt is easy to make, the simplicity of the design is quite versatile. Depending on the desired look of the finished quilt, endless color combinations will yield success.

The black and white, along with the checks and stripes, gives this variation an '80s vibe.

Note here how border treatments are also a design element to be considered. They truly change the overall look of the finished product.

Valentino Francine

Valentino Francine is a bright and cheerful quilt. This design showcases one of many graphic interpretations the blocks support. As in the Bauhaus Sampler, color placement is key to create the ombre effect. It's fun to play with multiple borders for this quilt, which enhances the optical energy of the finished piece.

Designed & pieced by Daisy Dodge • Quilted by Angie Vertucci
Quilt size: 62" x 57½" (157.5 x 146.1cm)

Materials

- Lemon fabric: 1¼ yards
- Chartreuse fabric: 1½ yards
- Meadow fabric: 1¾ yards
- Turquoise fabric: 1¾ yards
- Mint fabric: 1¾ yards
- Backing: 5 yards
- Batting: 5 yards
- Binding: ½ yard

Note: Yardage requirements are approximate, as these may vary depending on personal cutting/assembly technique.

Quilt Body Assembly

1. Piece the 156 blocks utilized in this quilt: 46 border blocks and 110 blocks for the body of the quilt. Using the charts on pages 34–36 and the Paper Piecing Basics on pages 12–15, piece the appropriate blocks in each color combination:

Color Combo 1: Lemon & Chartreuse . . . . 16 blocks

Color Combo 2: Chartreuse & Meadow . . . 20 blocks

Color Combo 3: Meadow & Turquoise . . . . 22 blocks

Color Combo 4: Turquoise & Mint . . . . 32 blocks

Color Combo 5: Meadow & Mint . . . . 20 blocks

Border Blocks: Colors as indicated . . . . 46 blocks

2. Once those are finished, separate them into stacks by color. This will make it easier to find each desired block for assembly.

3. Using the roadmap on page 37, arrange and assemble the blocks in horizontal rows. Sew the rows together, pressing seams flat as you go.

Adding the Border & Finishing the Quilt

1. Next, cut the borders and binding as follows:

Chartreuse Borders: 2" x 42" (5.1 x 106.7cm) . . . cut 6

Meadow Binding: 2¼" x 42" (5.7 x 106.7cm) . . . . cut 6

2. Utilizing the diagram below, attach the borders to the completed quilt body. The numbers correspond to the order in which you should attach each piece. Attach the top, then bottom; left then right.
   Note: You may wish to add additional borders to change the appearance or enlarge the quilt.

3. Layer the backing, batting, and quilt top. Baste, then quilt as desired.

4. Using the 2¼" (5.7cm)–wide strips, make and attach the binding to complete your masterpiece.

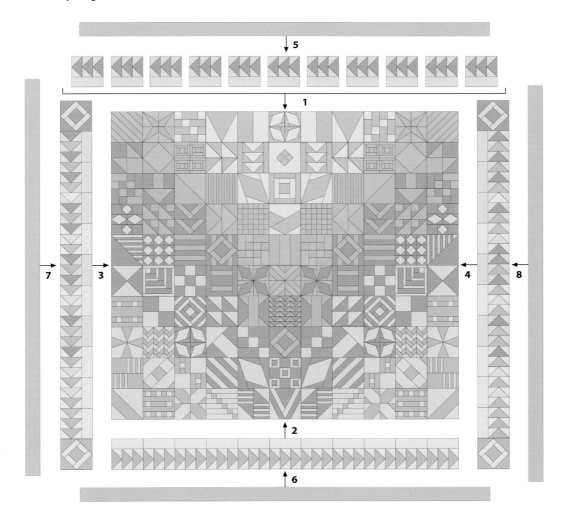

Color Combo 1

Using the following charts, make the required number
of each block in the color family as indicated.

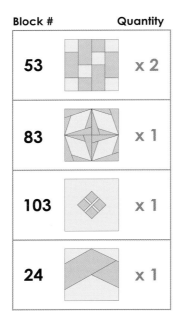

Block #		Quantity
53		x 2
83		x 1
103		x 1
24		x 1

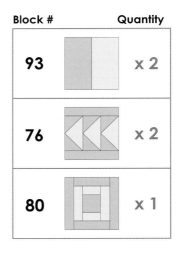

Block #		Quantity
97		x 2
57		x 2
31		x 2

Block #		Quantity
93		x 2
76		x 2
80		x 1

Color Combo 2

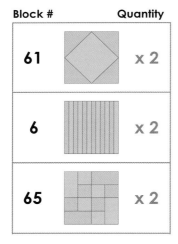

Block #		Quantity
61		x 2
6		x 2
65		x 2

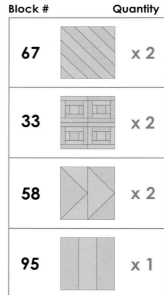

Block #		Quantity
67		x 2
33		x 2
58		x 2
95		x 1

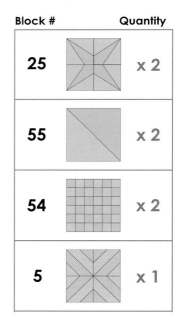

Block #		Quantity
25		x 2
55		x 2
54		x 2
5		x 1

Color Combo 3

Block #		Quantity	Block #		Quantity	Block #		Quantity
90	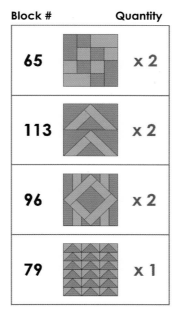	x 2	65		x 2	63		x 2
42		x 2	113		x 2	2		x 2
98		x 2	96		x 2	66		x 2
35		x 2	79		x 1	50		x 1

Color Combo 4

Block #		Quantity	Block #		Quantity	Block #		Quantity
49	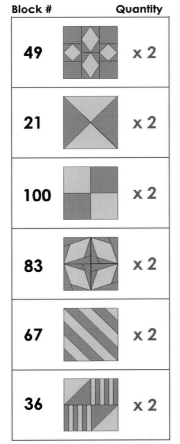	x 2	112	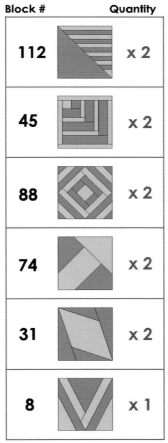	x 2	77	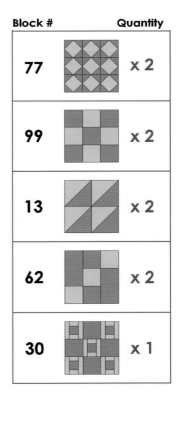	x 2
21		x 2	45		x 2	99		x 2
100		x 2	88		x 2	13		x 2
83		x 2	74		x 2	62		x 2
67		x 2	31		x 2	30		x 1
36		x 2	8		x 1			

Color Combo 5

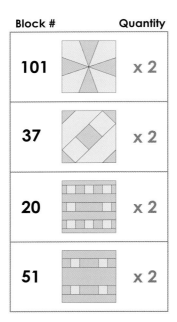
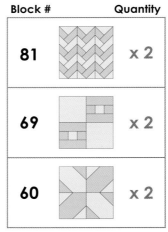
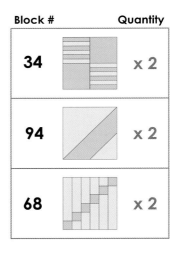

Block #	Quantity	Block #	Quantity	Block #	Quantity
101	x 2	81	x 2	34	x 2
37	x 2	69	x 2	94	x 2
20	x 2	60	x 2	68	x 2
51	x 2				

Border Blocks

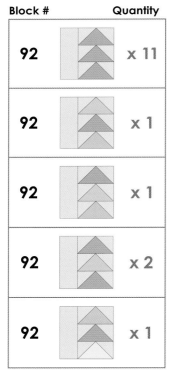
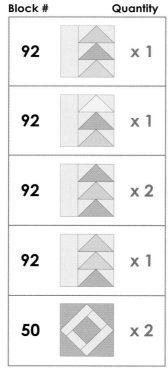
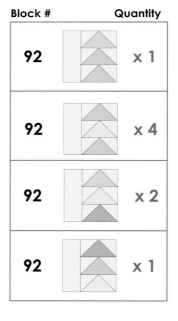
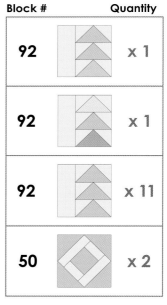

Block #	Quantity	Block #	Quantity	Block #	Quantity	Block #	Quantity
92	x 11	92	x 1	92	x 1	92	x 1
92	x 1	92	x 1	92	x 4	92	x 1
92	x 1	92	x 2	92	x 2	92	x 11
92	x 2	92	x 1	92	x 1	50	x 2
92	x 1	50	x 2				

Quilt Roadmap

Use this roadmap to facilitate block placement and quilt layout.
Numbers correspond to the block patterns presented in this book.

50	92	92	92	92	92	92	92	92	92	92	92	50
92	67	25	53	97	93	83	93	97	53	25	67	92
92	90	61	33	57	76	103	76	57	33	61	90	92
92	65	63	55	6	31	80	31	6	55	63	65	92
92	49	42	114	58	54	24	54	58	114	42	49	92
92	112	77	2	96	65	95	65	96	2	77	112	92
92	21	45	99	98	66	5	66	98	99	45	21	92
92	51	100	88	13	35	79	35	13	88	100	51	92
92	101	81	83	74	62	50	62	74	83	81	101	92
92	34	37	69	67	31	30	31	67	69	37	34	92
92	94	20	60	68	36	8	36	68	60	20	94	92
50	92	92	92	92	92	92	92	92	92	92	92	50

Treasure Island

Treasure Island is a bit more complex, as most blocks utilize more than two fabric colors. Although this is a more advanced design, the block construction remains the same no matter the quantity of colors in each. Take a trip to Treasure Island; the journey getting there is half the fun!

Designed & pieced by Daisy Dodge • Quilted by Angie Vertucci
Quilt size: 36" x 40½" (91.4 x 102.9cm)

Materials
- Peapod fabric: 1 yard
- Cornflower fabric: 1 yard
- Brown fabric: ⅜ yard
- Orange fabric: ⅜ yard
- Red fabric: ⅜ yard
- Backing: 3 yards
- Batting: 3 yards
- Binding: ⅜ yard

Note: Yardage requirements are approximate, as these may vary depending on personal cutting/assembly technique.

Quilt Body Assembly

1. Using the charts on pages 40–41 and following Paper Piecing Basics on pages 12–15, piece the indicated number of half-square triangle blocks in each color combination as indicated. I find it helpful to label each template with color placement. This will aid when piecing the blocks.

   Note: Remember the block templates are mirrored, so they are backwards from the final, desired direction.

2. Once the 72 blocks are complete, utilize the roadmap on page 42 as a guide. Lay them out on your design wall (or floor) to ensure correct placement and block direction.

3. Stack the blocks into nine piles, and begin making your nine assembled rows.

4. Assemble all rows, pressing seams as you go.

Finishing the Quilt

Although this quilt has no borders, you may choose to add one or more to your liking.

1. Cut and assemble the binding from the fabric:
   Cornflower: 2¼" x 42" (5.7 x 106.7cm) . . . . cut 5

2. Layer the backing, batting, and quilt top. Baste, then quilt as desired.

3. Using the 2¼" (5.7cm)–wide strips, make and attach the binding to complete your "compass" to Treasure Island.

Color Combos

Using the following charts, make the required number
of each block in the color family as indicated.

Block #		Quantity
80		x 1
80		x 1
11		x 1
66		x 2
66		x 1
6		x 1
31		x 1
27		x 1

Block #		Quantity
86		x 1
86		x 1
11		x 1
66		x 1
66		x 1
6		x 1
31		x 4
27		x 1

Block #		Quantity
81		x 1
81		x 2
98		x 1
66		x 1
92		x 1
6		x 1
90		x 2
27		x 1

Block #		Quantity	Block #		Quantity	Block #		Quantity
109		x 1	109		x 1	109		x 1
83		x 1	83		x 1	83		x 1
83		x 1	83		x 1	79		x 1
97		x 4	97		x 1	97		x 3
2		x 2	33		x 1	45		x 1
87		x 4	33		x 2	45		x 4
24		x 4	42		x 1	42		x 1
102		x 1	42		x 1	42		x 1
102		x 1	89		x 1			

Quilt Roadmap

Use this roadmap to facilitate block placement and quilt layout.
Numbers correspond to the block patterns presented in this book.

80	81	81	86	102	11	66	66
97	109	2	90	98	6	66	66
86	83	83	33	97	27	109	92
6	83	83	27	45	24	87	83
90	79	109	87	31	97	31	45
33	45	6	24	97	66	97	24
42	42	102	45	31	97	31	87
42	42	11	89	87	24	45	33
81	31	80	97	66	2	27	97

Treasure Island Color Variations

Explore alternate ways to use color for this quilt. Be daring with your palette choices!

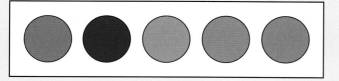

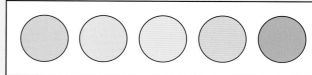

THE BLOCKS

Each block design on the following pages, identified by name and number, are presented with templates and directions for both foundation paper piecing (FPP) and traditional piecing methods.

For FPP, you will need to photocopy the templates in the book. The roadmap charts for each quilt indicate the appropriate quantity for that block. For example, in the quilt Valentino Francine, you need two copies of Block 53; assemble with the colors placed as shown in the diagram.

All of the projects and blocks in the book can also be accomplished with traditional piecing. Patterns are located at the end of this section. If you wish to cut traditional piece patterns for your assembly, utilize the cutting charts on each page, which will indicate how many of each template piece you will need to trace for each block. You will still need to reference the roadmap chart to dictate piece color and block quantity for each quilt project.

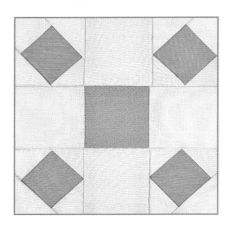

TRADITIONAL PIECING

Numbers on diagram indicate the template number (see chart). See templates on pages 157, 159, 164.

	Cut Qty	Template #
■	5	43
▲	16	44
◆	4	45

PAPER PIECING

Numbers indicate the piecing order.

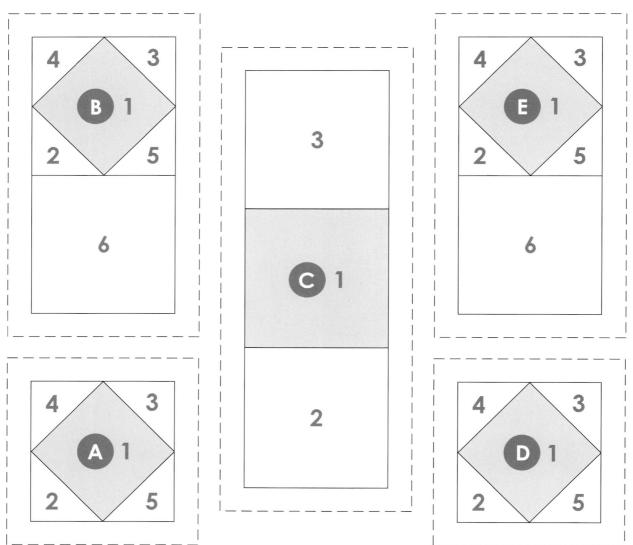

TRADITIONAL PIECING

Numbers on diagram indicate the template number (see chart). See template on page 157.

	Cut Qty	Template #
	6	73

73

73
73
73
73
73

PAPER PIECING

Numbers indicate the piecing order.

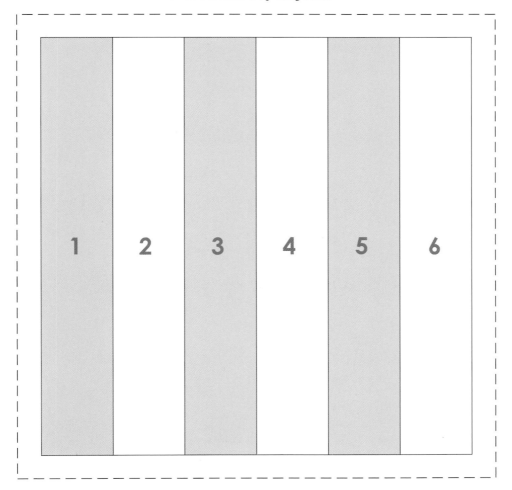

1 2 3 4 5 6

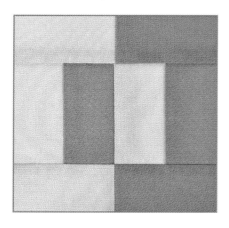

TRADITIONAL PIECING

Numbers on diagram indicate the template number (see chart). See templates on pages 157, 168.

	Cut Qty	Template #
	2	77
	2	57
	4	61

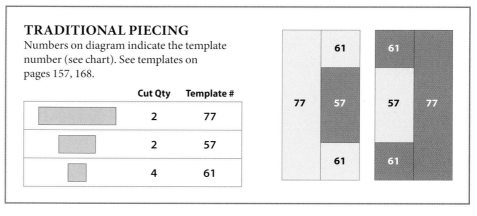

PAPER PIECING

Numbers indicate the piecing order.

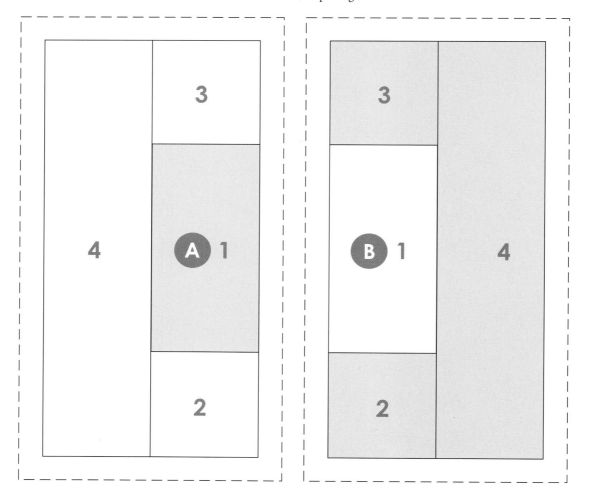

TRADITIONAL PIECING

Numbers on diagram indicate the template number (see chart). See templates on pages 157, 159, 160, 164.

	Cut Qty	Template #
▢	4	43
◣	16	44
◆	4	45
▲	2	5
◇	1	59
⬠	2	60

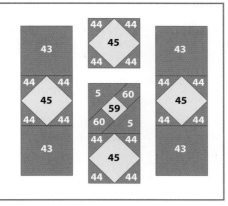

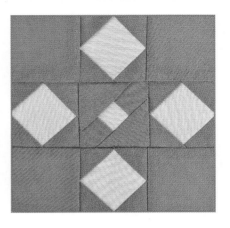

PAPER PIECING
Numbers indicate the piecing order.

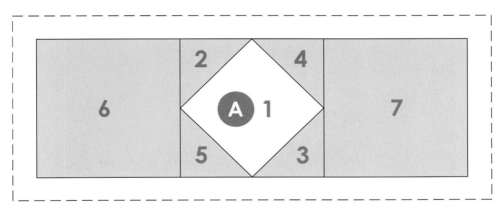

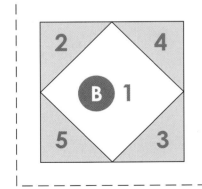

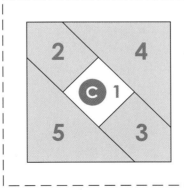

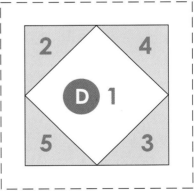

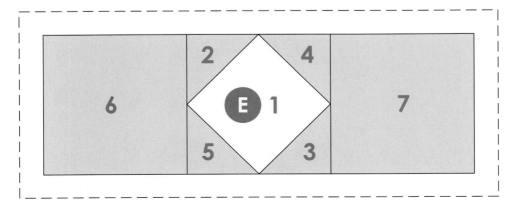

TRADITIONAL PIECING

Numbers on diagram indicate the template number (see chart). See templates on pages 160–61.

	Cut Qty	Template #
	8	5
	8	6

PAPER PIECING
Numbers indicate the piecing order.

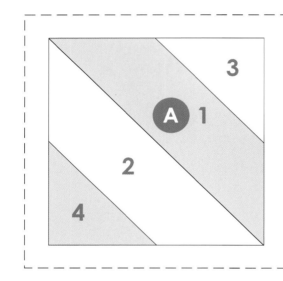
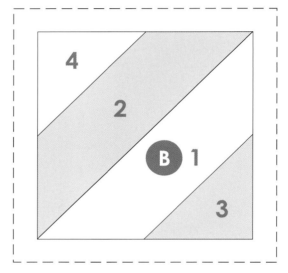
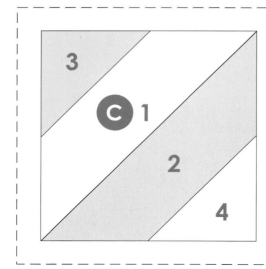
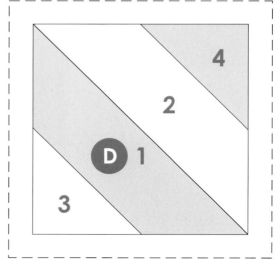

TRADITIONAL PIECING

Numbers on diagram indicate the template number (see chart). See template on page 159.

	Cut Qty	Template #
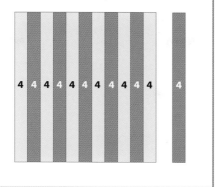	12	4

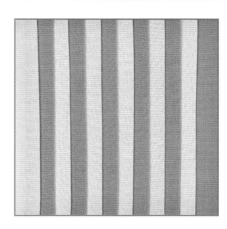

PAPER PIECING

Numbers indicate the piecing order.

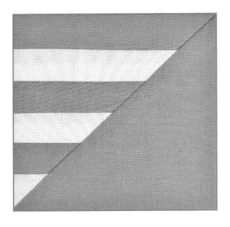

TRADITIONAL PIECING

Numbers on diagram indicate the template number (see chart). See templates on pages 161–65.

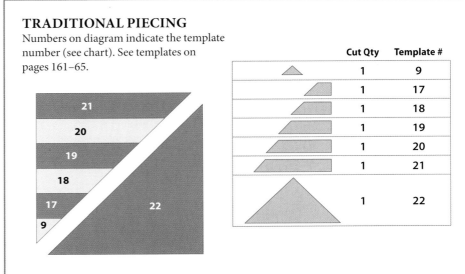

	Cut Qty	Template #
	1	9
	1	17
	1	18
	1	19
	1	20
	1	21
	1	22

PAPER PIECING

Numbers indicate the piecing order.

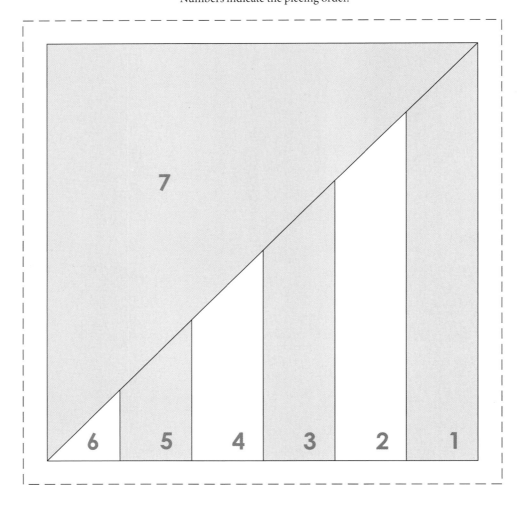

TRADITIONAL PIECING

Numbers on diagram indicate the template number (see chart). See templates on page 172.

	Cut Qty	Template #
	1	112
	1	113
	1	115
	1	116
	1	111
	1	117
	1	114

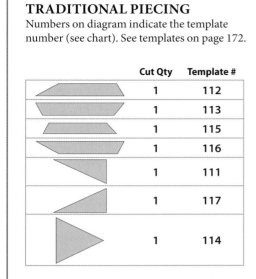

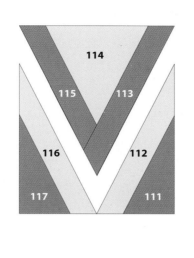

PAPER PIECING

Numbers indicate the piecing order.

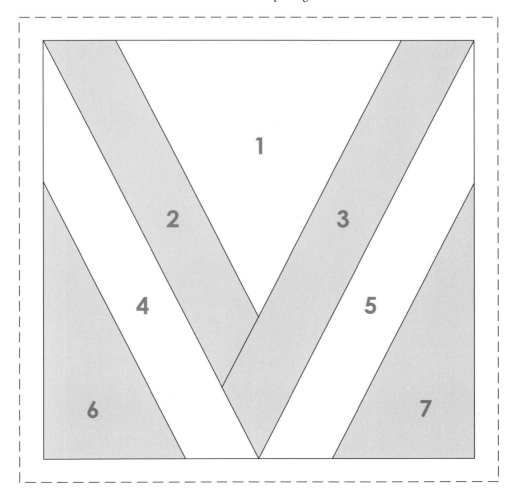

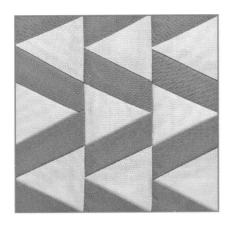

TRADITIONAL PIECING

Numbers on diagram indicate the template number (see chart). See templates on pages 168, 172.

	Cut Qty	Template #
	3	47
	3	49
	9	48
	3	119
	3	120

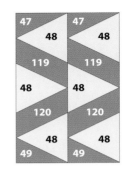 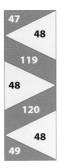

PAPER PIECING

Numbers indicate the piecing order.

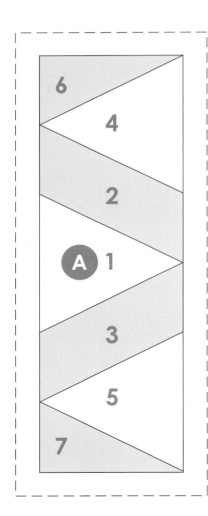 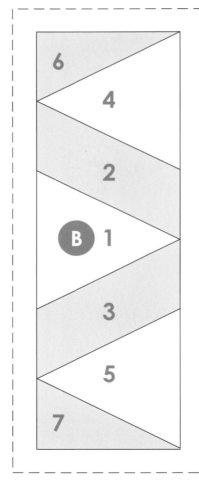 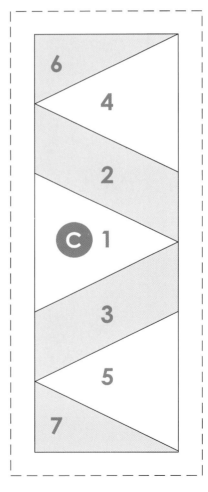

TRADITIONAL PIECING

Numbers on diagram indicate the template number (see chart). See templates on pages 157, 159.

	Cut Qty	Template #
	2	73
	8	81
	2	43

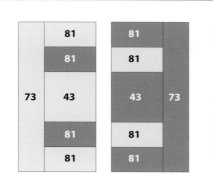

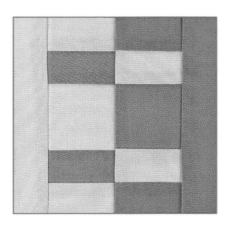

PAPER PIECING

Numbers indicate the piecing order.

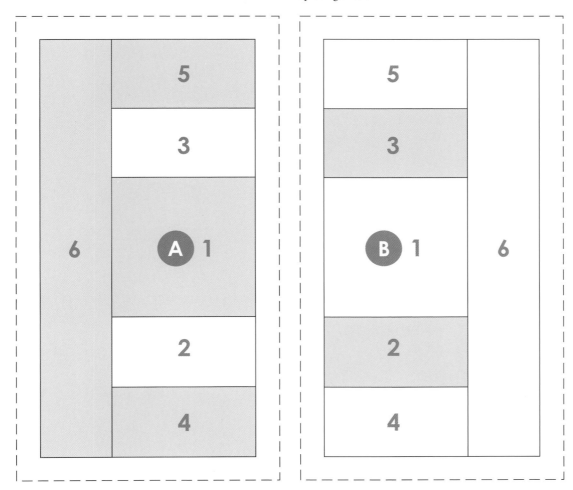

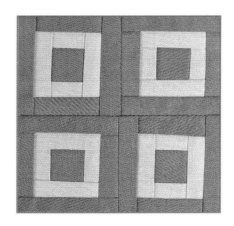

TRADITIONAL PIECING

Numbers on diagram indicate the template number (see chart). See templates on pages 157–59.

	Cut Qty	Template #
	4	86
	8	1
	16	2
	8	3

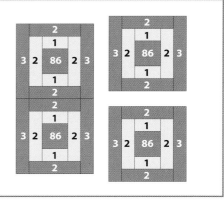

PAPER PIECING

Numbers indicate the piecing order.

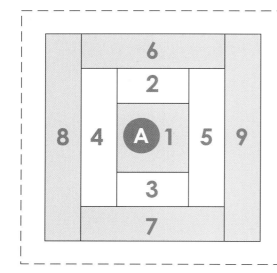

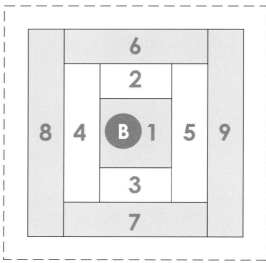

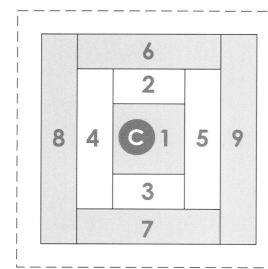

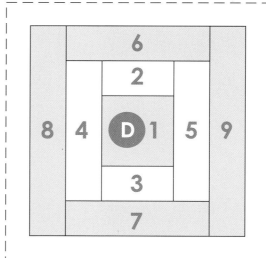

TRADITIONAL PIECING

Numbers on diagram indicate the template number (see chart). See templates on pages 159–60, 164, 167.

	Cut Qty	Template #
◿	8	5
◣	4	28
▱	2	29
▱	2	30
▢	1	31

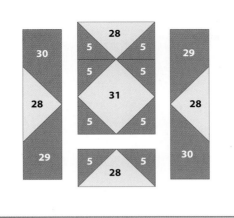

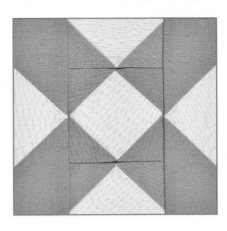

PAPER PIECING

Numbers indicate the piecing order.

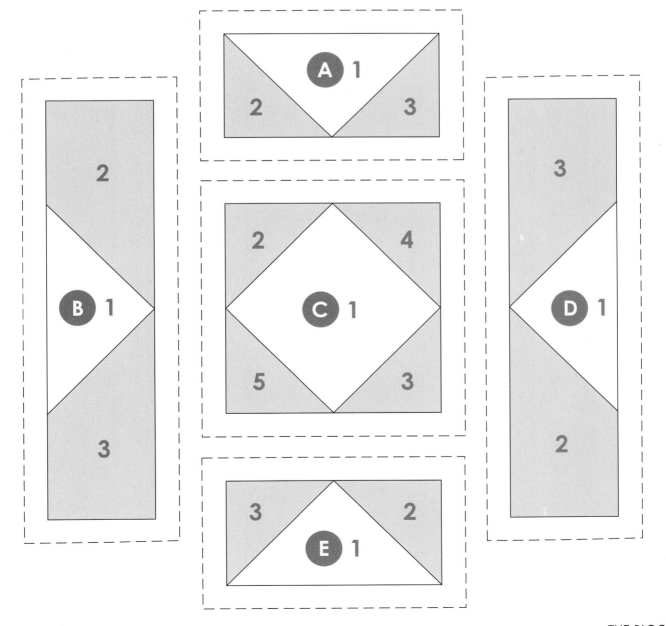

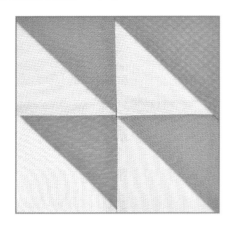

TRADITIONAL PIECING

Numbers on diagram indicate the template number (see chart). See template on page 166.

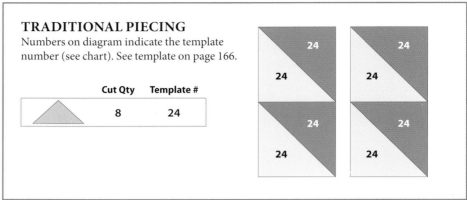

	Cut Qty	Template #
▲	8	24

PAPER PIECING

Numbers indicate the piecing order.

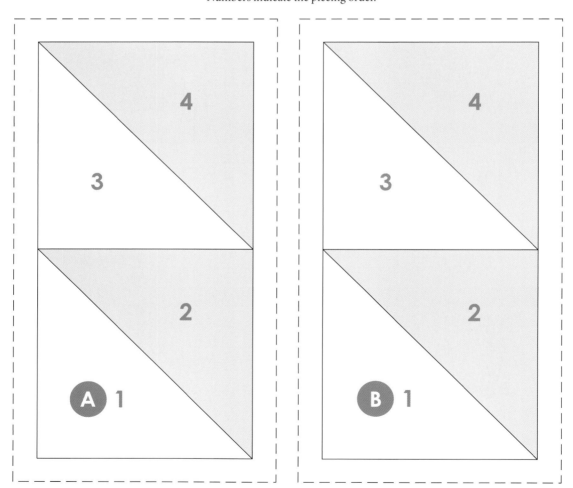

TRADITIONAL PIECING

Numbers on diagram indicate the template number (see chart). See templates on pages 166, 168.

	Cut Qty	Template #
	2	71
	2	57
	4	70

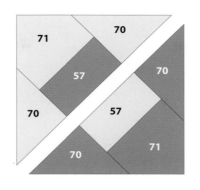

PAPER PIECING

Numbers indicate the piecing order.

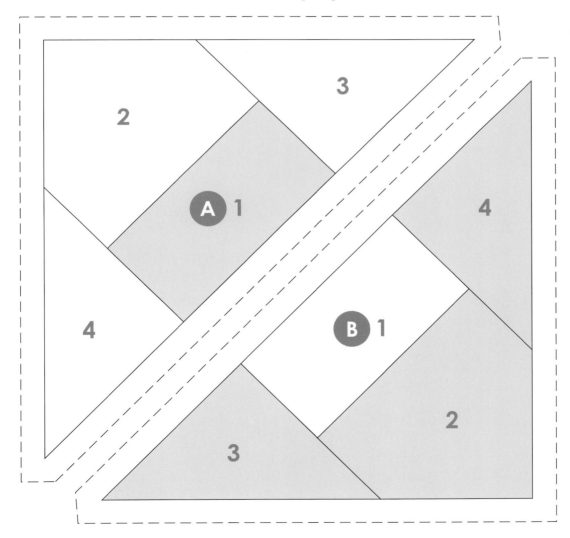

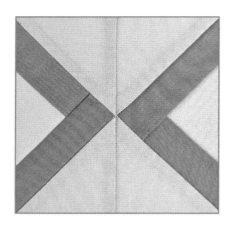

TRADITIONAL PIECING

Numbers on diagram indicate the template number (see chart). See templates on pages 160, 166.

	Cut Qty	Template #
	2	83
	2	84
	2	85
	4	24

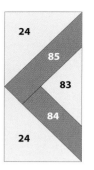

PAPER PIECING

Numbers indicate the piecing order.

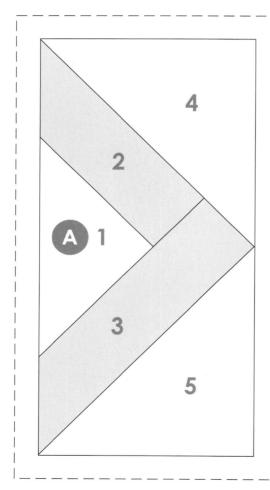
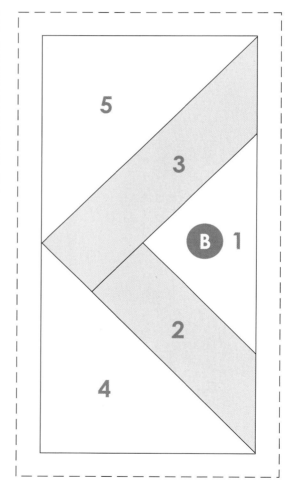

TRADITIONAL PIECING

Numbers on diagram indicate the template number (see chart). See templates on pages 160, 166.

	Cut Qty	Template #
	2	68
	2	69
	2	70

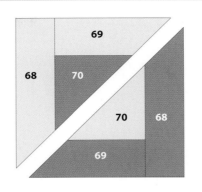

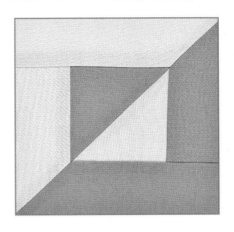

PAPER PIECING

Numbers indicate the piecing order.

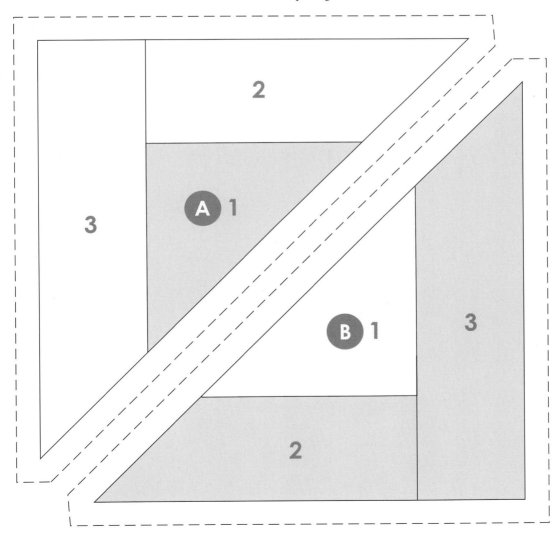

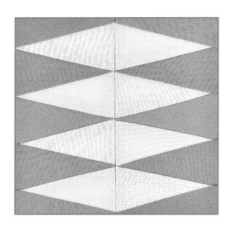

TRADITIONAL PIECING

Numbers on diagram indicate the template number (see chart). See templates on pages 167, 170.

	Cut Qty	Template #
	14	39
	2	40
	2	55

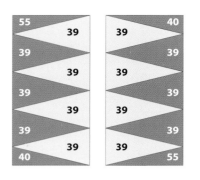

PAPER PIECING

Numbers indicate the piecing order.

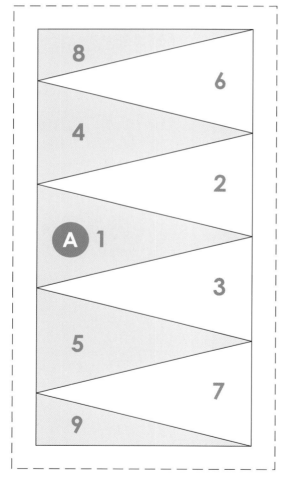

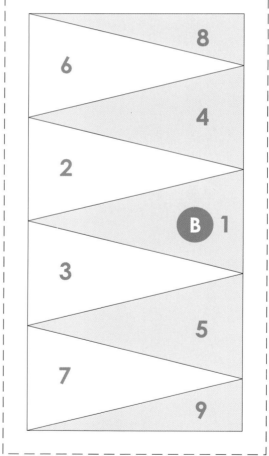

TRADITIONAL PIECING

Numbers on diagram indicate the template number (see chart). See templates on pages 165–66.

	Cut Qty	Template #
	2	24
	2	26
	1	27

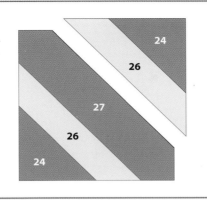

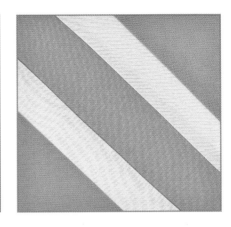

PAPER PIECING

Numbers indicate the piecing order.

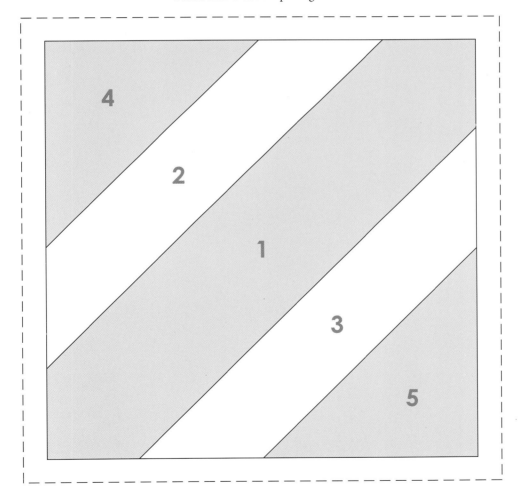

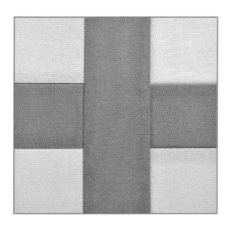

TRADITIONAL PIECING

Numbers on diagram indicate the template number (see chart). See templates on pages 157, 159.

	Cut Qty	Template #
	6	43
	1	56

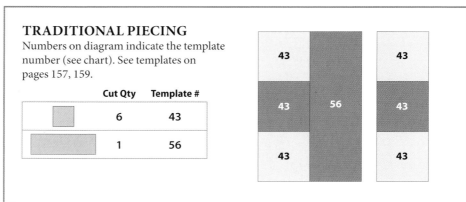

PAPER PIECING

Numbers indicate the piecing order.

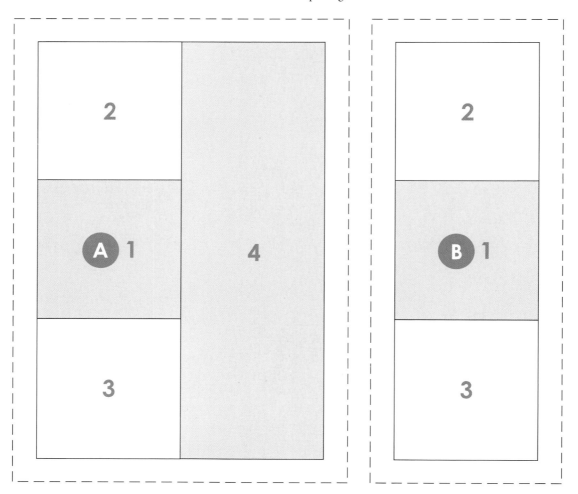

TRADITIONAL PIECING

Numbers on diagram indicate the template number (see chart). See templates on pages 157, 159, 168.

	Cut Qty	Template #
	12	86
	6	1
	2	73
	1	88
	2	4

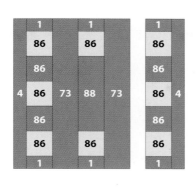

PAPER PIECING

Numbers indicate the piecing order.

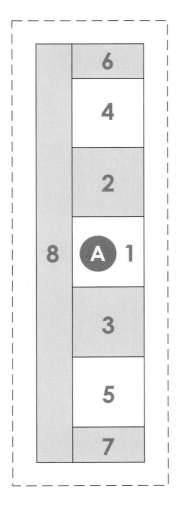

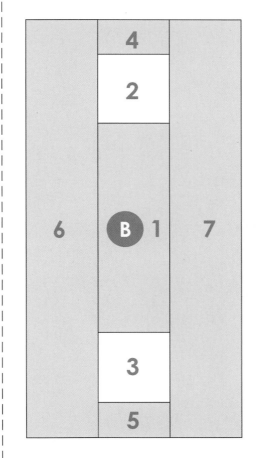

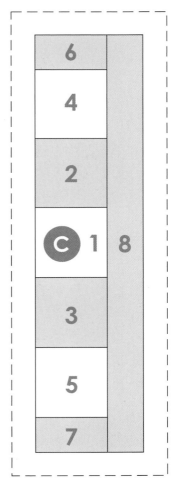

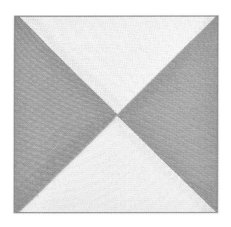

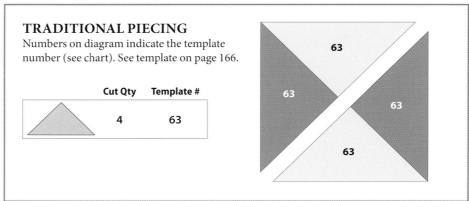

TRADITIONAL PIECING

Numbers on diagram indicate the template number (see chart). See template on page 166.

	Cut Qty	Template #
▲	4	63

PAPER PIECING

Numbers indicate the piecing order.

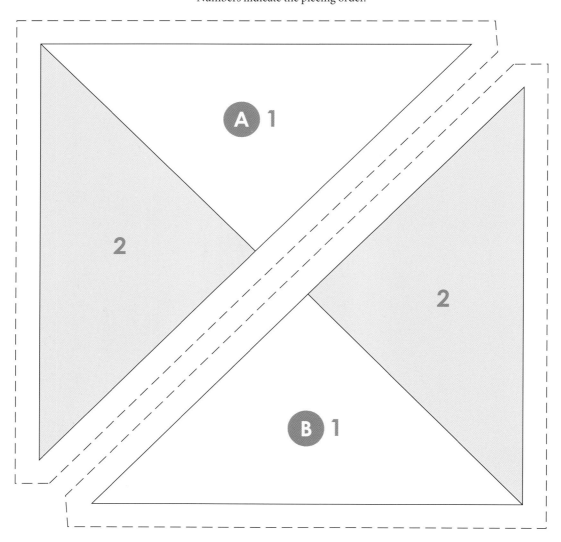

TRADITIONAL PIECING

Numbers on diagram indicate the template number (see chart). See templates on pages 164, 166.

	Cut Qty	Template #
▲	2	24
⬡	1	25

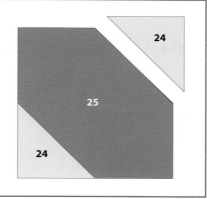

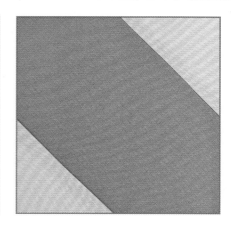

PAPER PIECING

Numbers indicate the piecing order.

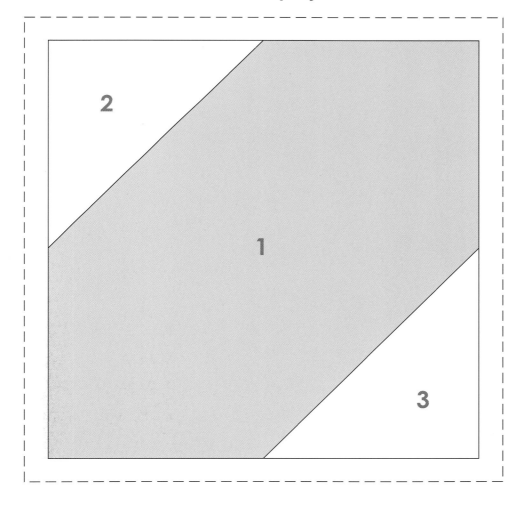

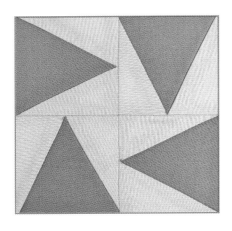

TRADITIONAL PIECING

Numbers on diagram indicate the template number (see chart). See templates on pages 167, 171.

	Cut Qty	Template #
	4	96
	4	97
	4	98

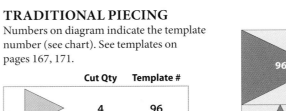

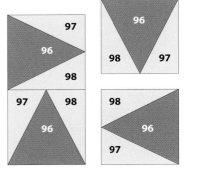

PAPER PIECING

Numbers indicate the piecing order.

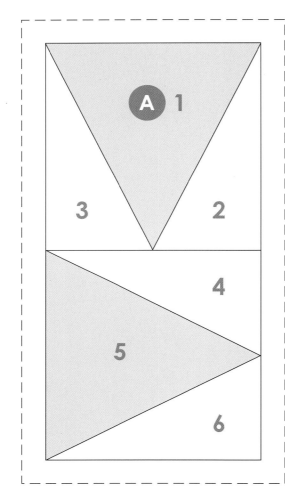

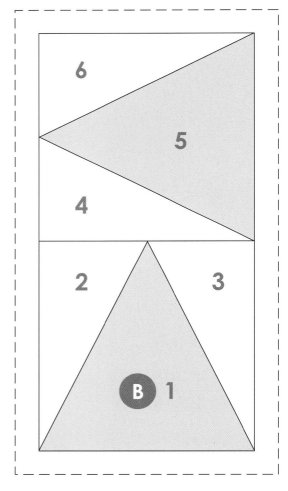

TRADITIONAL PIECING

Numbers on diagram indicate the template number (see chart). See templates on pages 163, 169, 171.

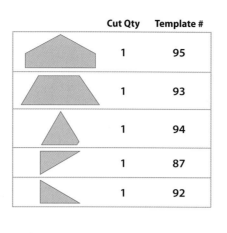

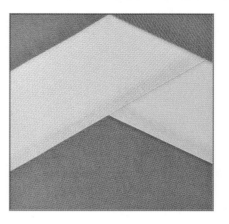

	Cut Qty	Template #
	1	95
	1	93
	1	94
	1	87
	1	92

PAPER PIECING

Numbers indicate the piecing order.

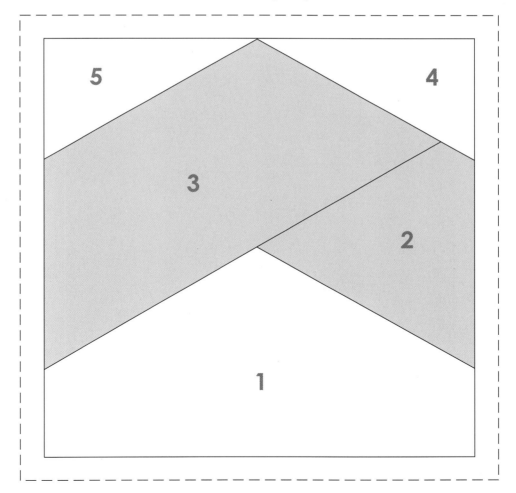

TRADITIONAL PIECING

Numbers on diagram indicate the template number (see chart). See templates on pages 162, 172.

	Cut Qty	Template #
	4	103
	4	104
	4	105

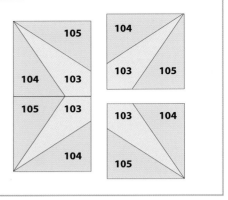

PAPER PIECING

Numbers indicate the piecing order.

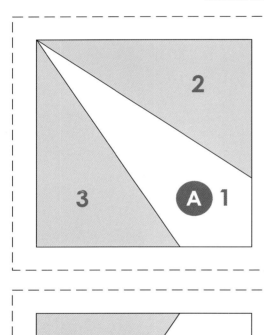

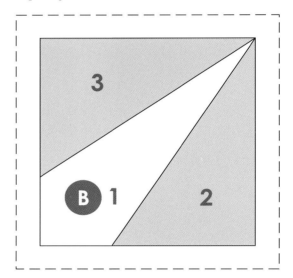

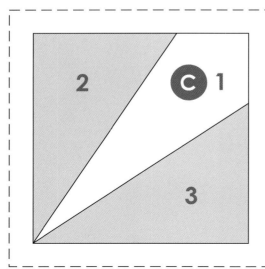

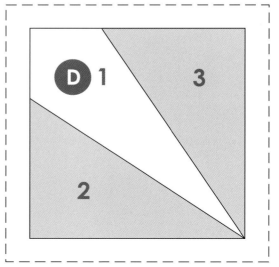

TRADITIONAL PIECING

Numbers on diagram indicate the template number (see chart). See templates on pages 159–60.

	Cut Qty	Template #
▲	16	5
■	4	31

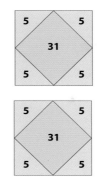
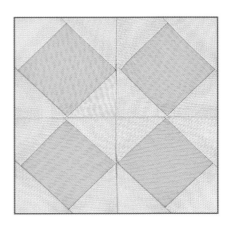

PAPER PIECING
Numbers indicate the piecing order.

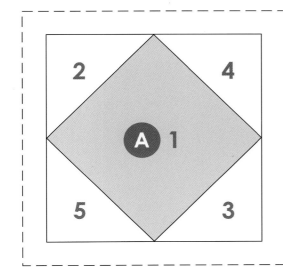
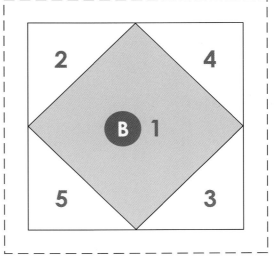
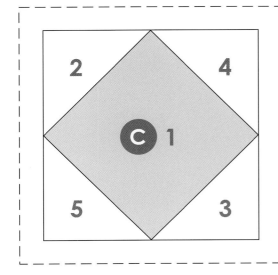
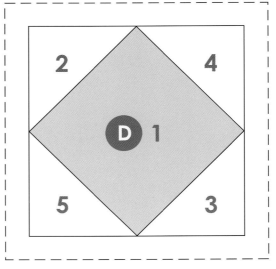

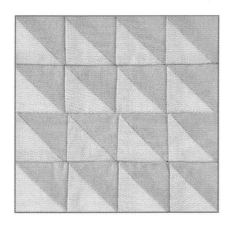

TRADITIONAL PIECING

Numbers on diagram indicate the template number (see chart). See template on page 160.

	Cut Qty	Template #
◺	32	5

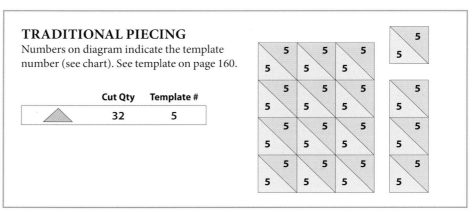

PAPER PIECING

Numbers indicate the piecing order.

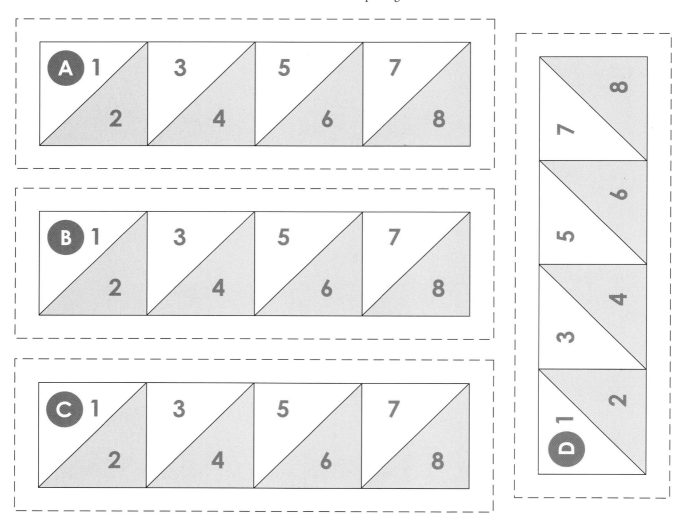

TRADITIONAL PIECING

Numbers on diagram indicate the template number (see chart). See templates on pages 166–67.

Cut Qty	Template #
4	97
4	98
4	75

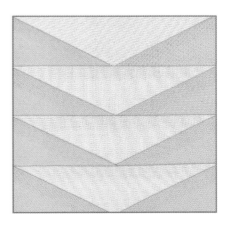

PAPER PIECING

Numbers indicate the piecing order.

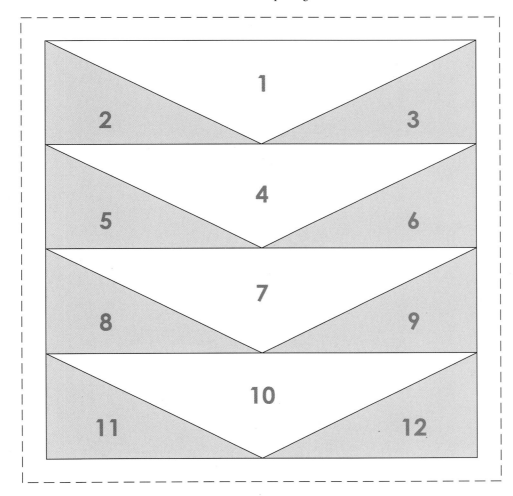

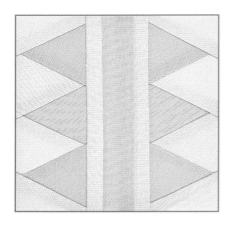

TRADITIONAL PIECING

Numbers on diagram indicate the template number (see chart). See templates on pages 157, 159, 168.

	Cut Qty	Template #
	2	47
	2	49
	10	48
	2	4
	1	73

PAPER PIECING

Numbers indicate the piecing order.

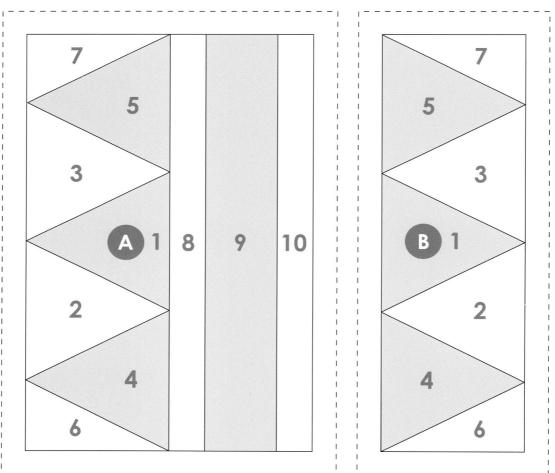

TRADITIONAL PIECING

Numbers on diagram indicate the template number (see chart). See templates on pages 157–59.

	Cut Qty	Template #
	5	86
	10	1
	10	2
	4	43

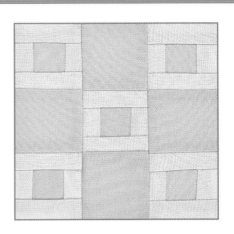

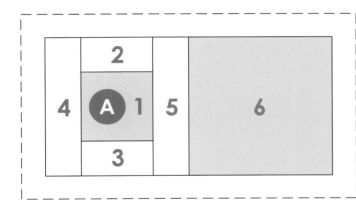

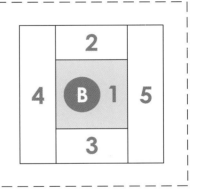

PAPER PIECING

Numbers indicate the piecing order.

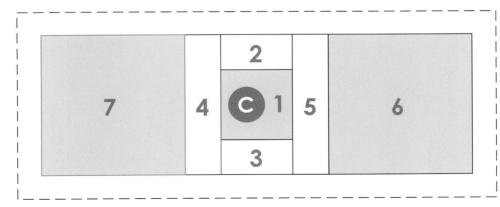

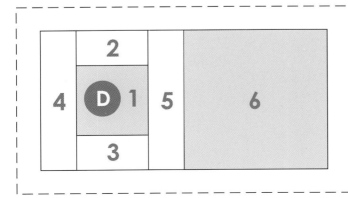

TRADITIONAL PIECING

Numbers on diagram indicate the template number (see chart). See templates on pages 162, 169.

	Cut Qty	Template #
	2	36
	2	37
	1	38

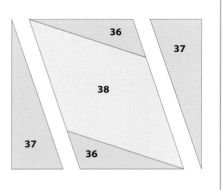

PAPER PIECING

Numbers indicate the piecing order.

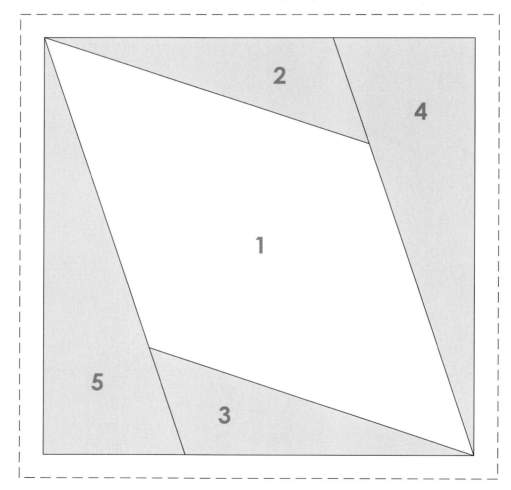

TRADITIONAL PIECING

Numbers on diagram indicate the template number (see chart). See templates on pages 167–68, 171.

	Cut Qty	Template #
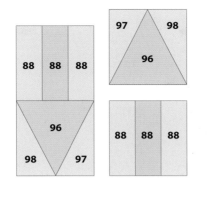	2	96
	2	97
	2	98
	6	88

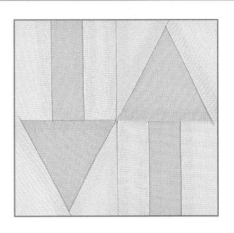

PAPER PIECING

Numbers indicate the piecing order.

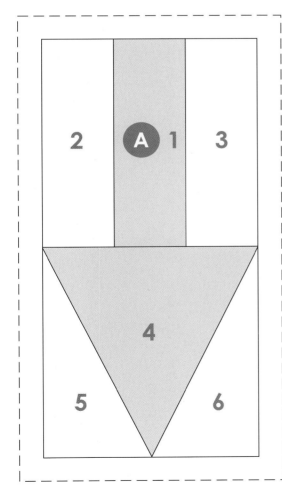

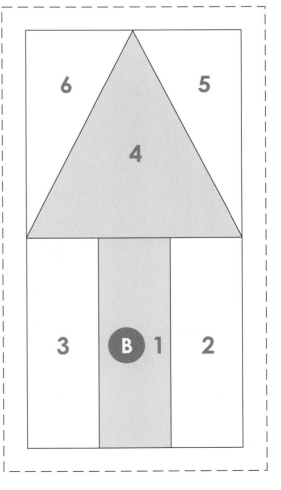

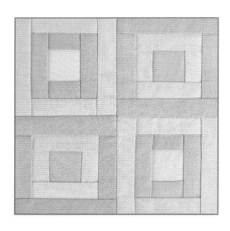

TRADITIONAL PIECING

Numbers on diagram indicate the template number (see chart). See templates on pages 157–59.

	Cut Qty	Template #
	4	86
	8	1
	16	2
	8	3

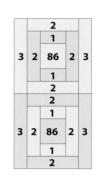

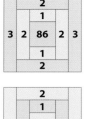

PAPER PIECING

Numbers indicate the piecing order.

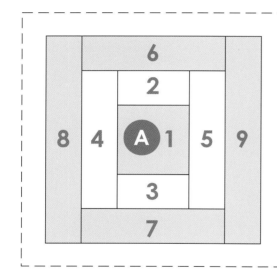

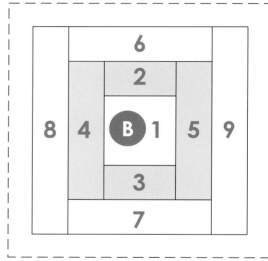

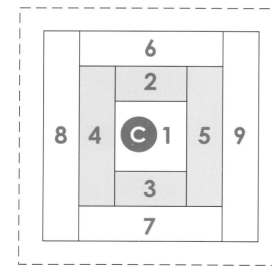

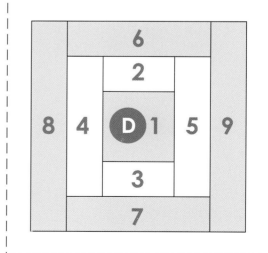

TRADITIONAL PIECING

Numbers on diagram indicate the template number (see chart). See templates on pages 159, 168.

	Cut Qty	Template #
	12	3
	2	62

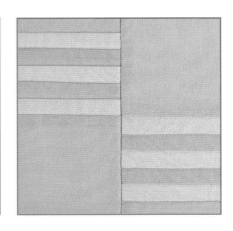

PAPER PIECING

Numbers indicate the piecing order.

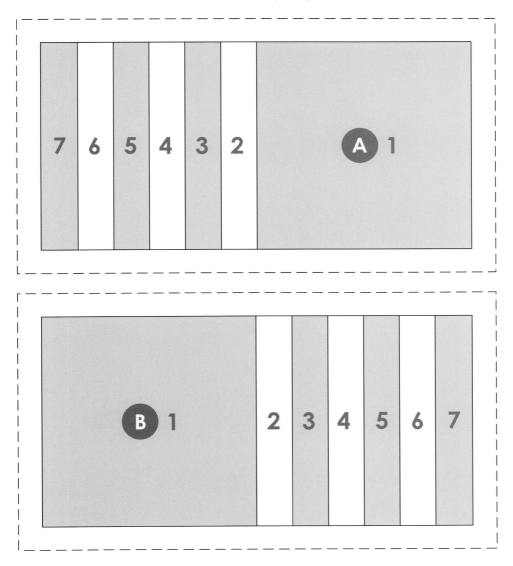

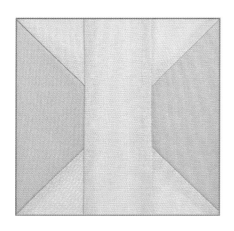

TRADITIONAL PIECING

Numbers on diagram indicate the template number (see chart). See templates on pages 157, 160, 162.

	Cut Qty	Template #
	4	74
	2	99
	1	56

PAPER PIECING

Numbers indicate the piecing order.

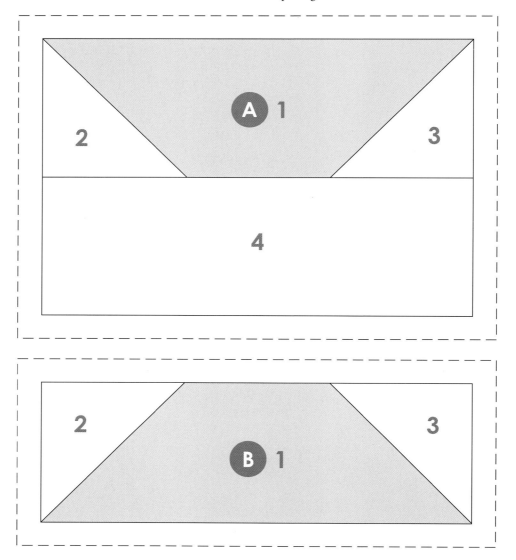

TRADITIONAL PIECING

Numbers on diagram indicate the template number (see chart). See templates on pages 159, 166.

	Cut Qty	Template #
▭	12	3
▲	4	24

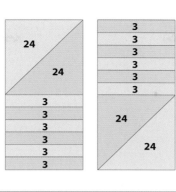

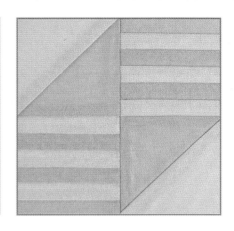

PAPER PIECING

Numbers indicate the piecing order.

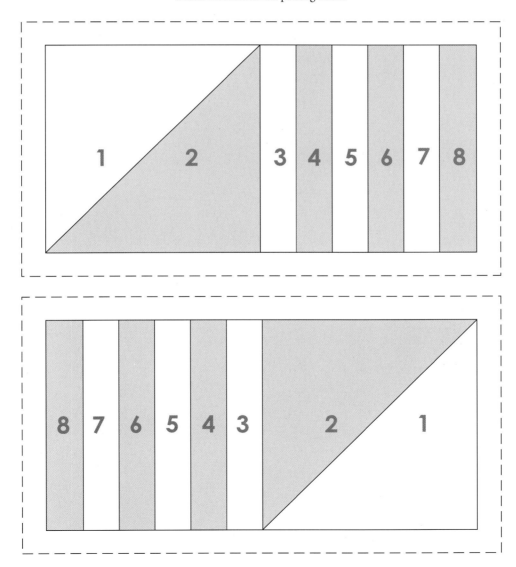

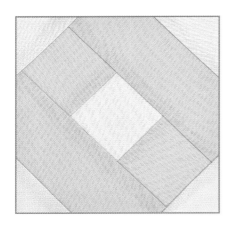

TRADITIONAL PIECING

Numbers on diagram indicate the template number (see chart). See templates on pages 159–60, 165.

	Cut Qty	Template #
△	4	5
◻	3	31
⬟	2	169

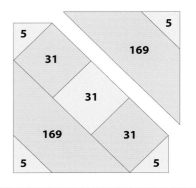

PAPER PIECING

Numbers indicate the piecing order.

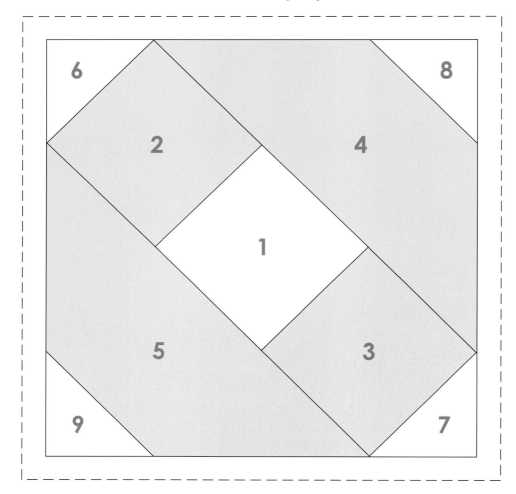

TRADITIONAL PIECING

Numbers on diagram indicate the template number (see chart). See templates on page 170.

	Cut Qty	Template #
	2	64
	2	65

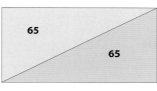

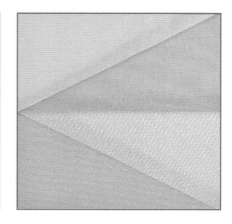

PAPER PIECING

Numbers indicate the piecing order.

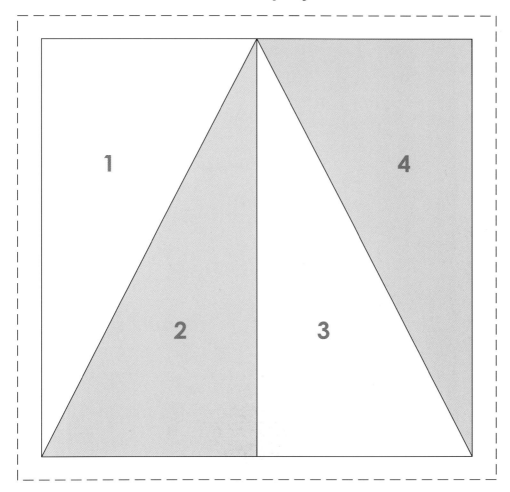

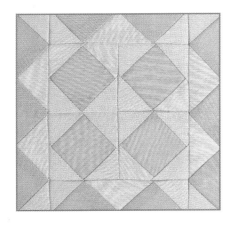

TRADITIONAL PIECING

Numbers on diagram indicate the template number (see chart). See templates on pages 157, 164, 166.

	Cut Qty	Template #
◺	24	44
◇	4	45
◿	16	76

PAPER PIECING

Numbers indicate the piecing order.

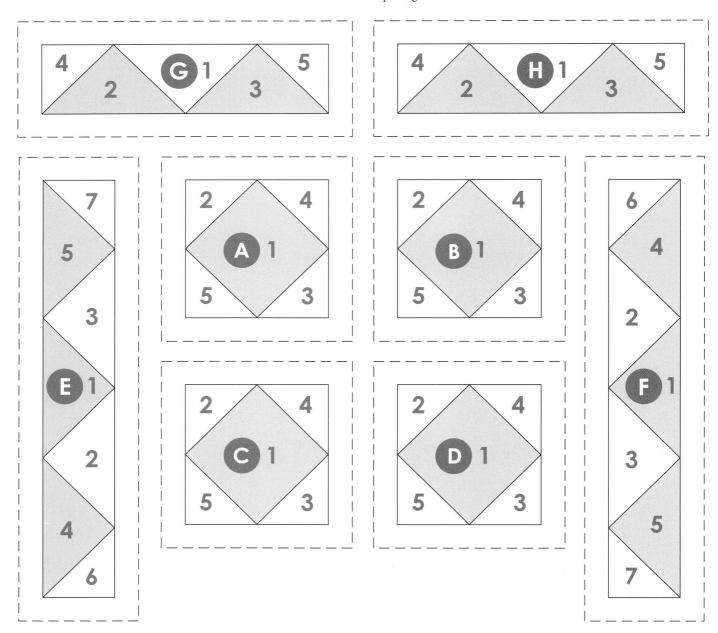

TRADITIONAL PIECING

Numbers on diagram indicate the template number (see chart). See templates on pages 160, 164, 167–68.

	Cut Qty	Template #
	4	28
	2	29
	2	30
	1	62
	4	5

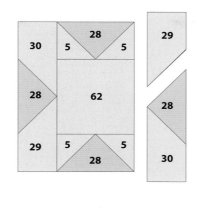

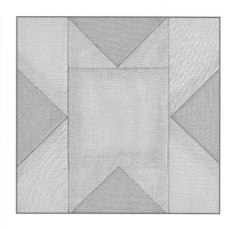

PAPER PIECING

Numbers indicate the piecing order.

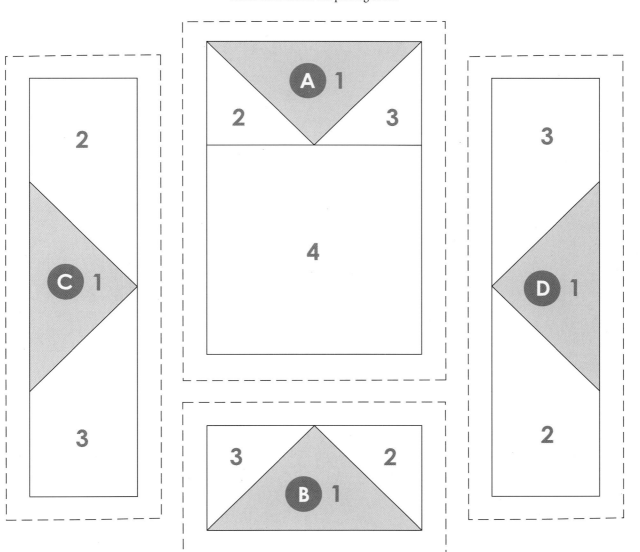

TRADITIONAL PIECING

Numbers on diagram indicate the template number (see chart). See templates on page 162.

	Cut Qty	Template #
	1	107
	1	108
	7	106

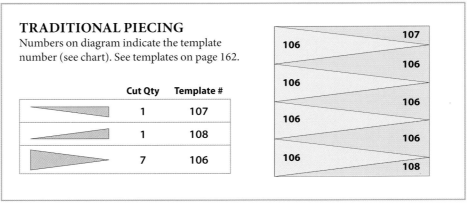

PAPER PIECING

Numbers indicate the piecing order.

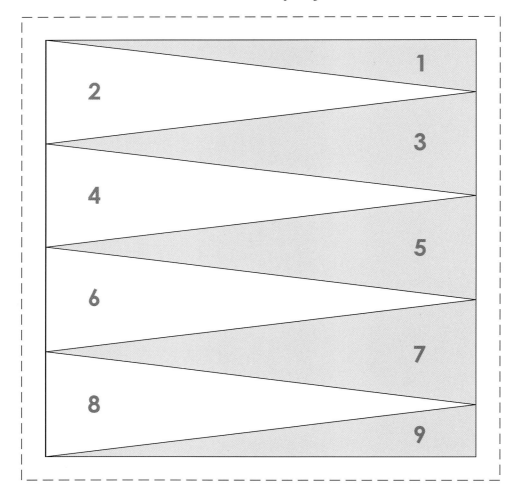

TRADITIONAL PIECING

Numbers on diagram indicate the template number (see chart). See templates on pages 157, 160, 166.

	Cut Qty	Template #
▲	8	5
■	4	61
▲	4	24

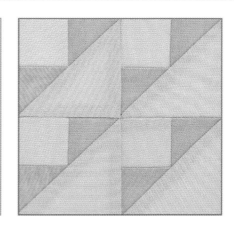

PAPER PIECING

Numbers indicate the piecing order.

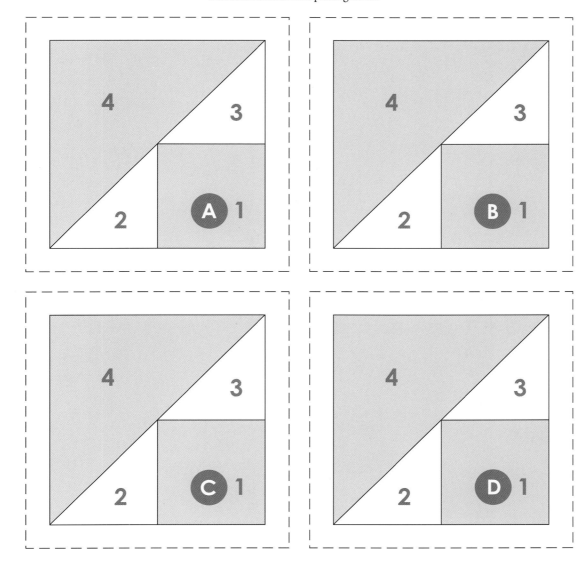

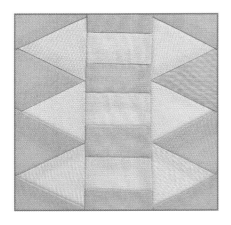

TRADITIONAL PIECING

Numbers on diagram indicate the template number (see chart). See templates on pages 158–59, 168.

	Cut Qty	Template #
◢	2	47
◣	2	49
▲	10	48
▭	5	81
▬	2	2

49		2		49
	48	81	48	
48		81		48
	48	81	48	
48		81		48
	48	81	48	
47		2		47

PAPER PIECING

Numbers indicate the piecing order.

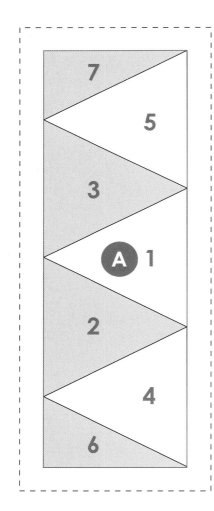

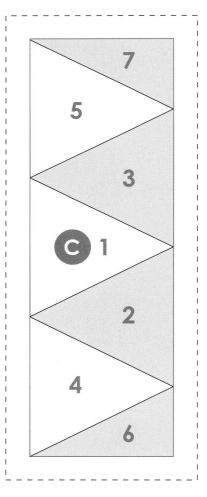

TRADITIONAL PIECING

Numbers on diagram indicate the template number (see chart). See templates on pages 160, 166.

	Cut Qty	Template #
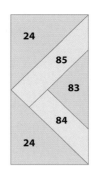	2	83
	2	84
	2	85
	4	24

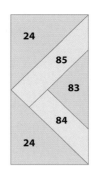

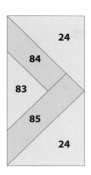

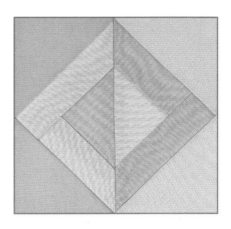

PAPER PIECING
Numbers indicate the piecing order.

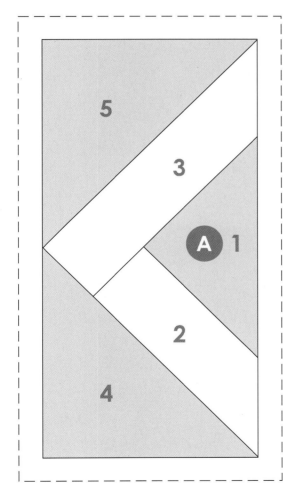

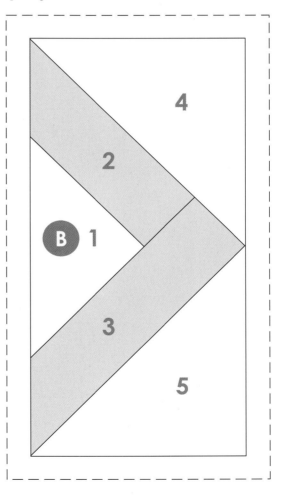

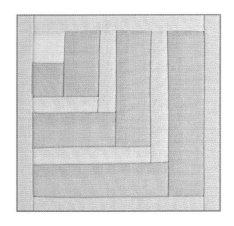

TRADITIONAL PIECING

Numbers on diagram indicate the template number (see chart). See templates on pages 157–59.

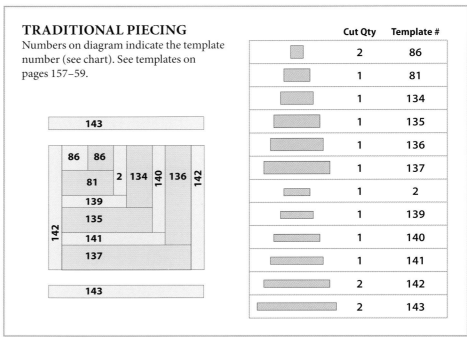

	Cut Qty	Template #
	2	86
	1	81
	1	134
	1	135
	1	136
	1	137
	1	2
	1	139
	1	140
	1	141
	2	142
	2	143

PAPER PIECING

Numbers indicate the piecing order.

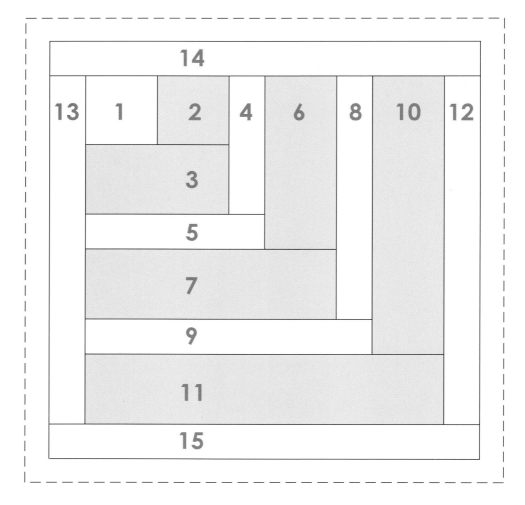

TRADITIONAL PIECING

Numbers on diagram indicate the template number (see chart). See templates on pages 160, 162, 166.

	Cut Qty	Template #
	8	5
	6	121
	6	144

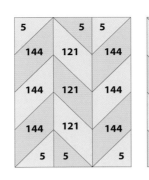

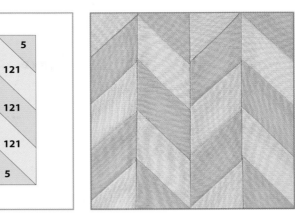

PAPER PIECING

Numbers indicate the piecing order.

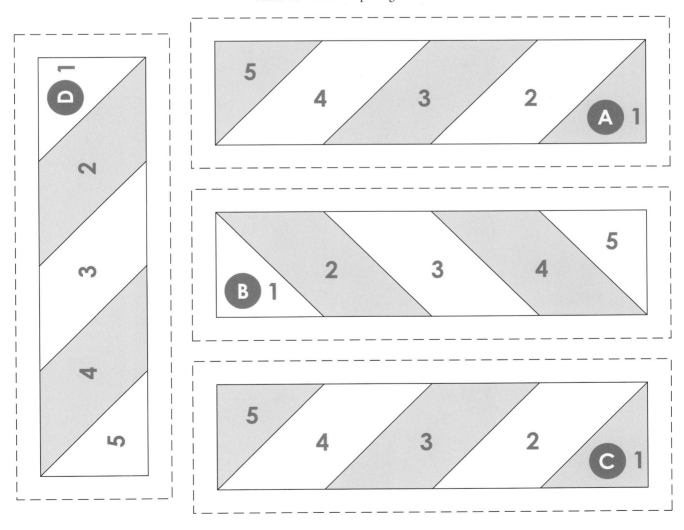

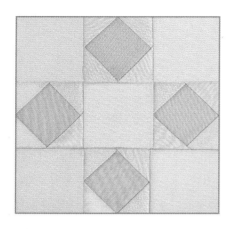

TRADITIONAL PIECING

Numbers on diagram indicate the template number (see chart). See templates on pages 157, 159, 164.

	Cut Qty	Template #
◻	5	43
◢	16	44
◆	4	45

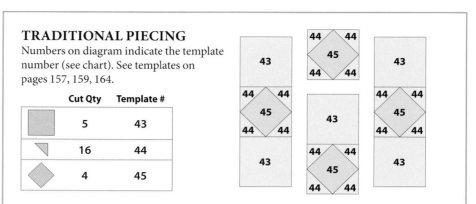

PAPER PIECING

Numbers indicate the piecing order.

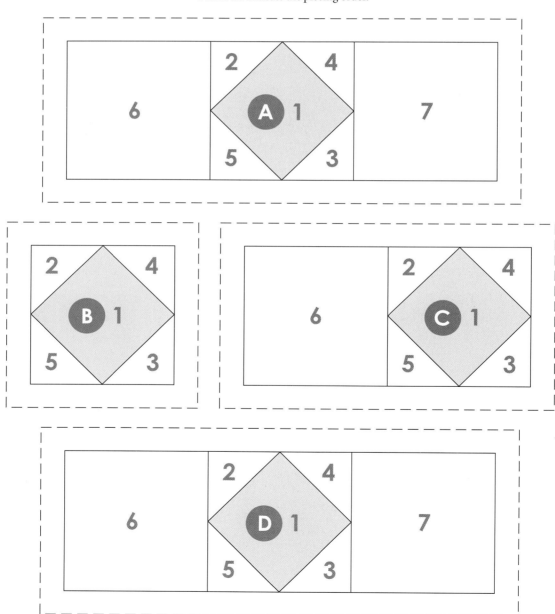

TRADITIONAL PIECING

Numbers on diagram indicate the template number (see chart). See templates on pages 166–67.

	Cut Qty	Template #
	4	97
	4	98
	2	75
	1	109

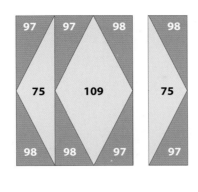

PAPER PIECING

Numbers indicate the piecing order.

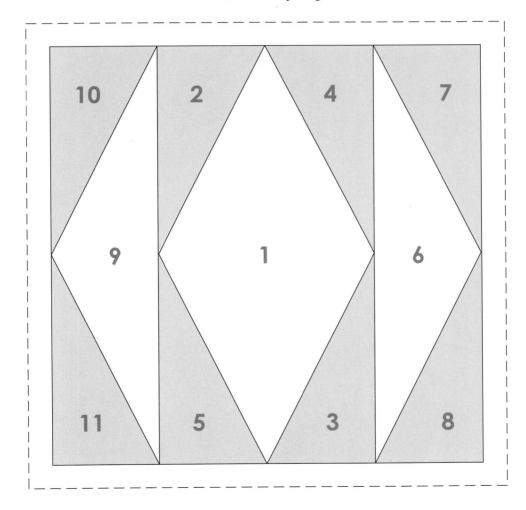

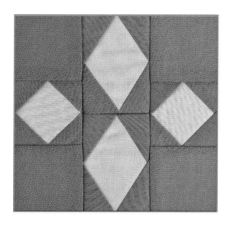

TRADITIONAL PIECING

Numbers on diagram indicate the template number (see chart). See templates on pages 157, 159, 164, 169–70.

	Cut Qty	Template #
	2	41
	4	42
	4	43
	8	44
	2	45
	4	46

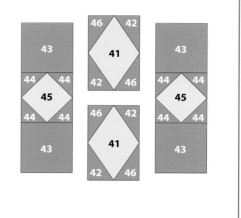

PAPER PIECING

Numbers indicate the piecing order.

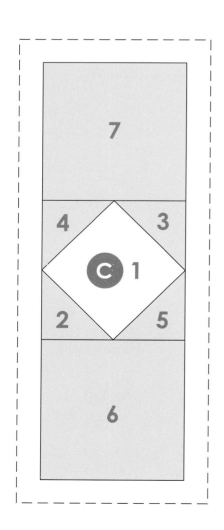

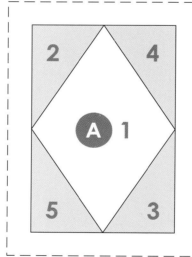

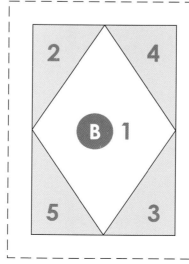

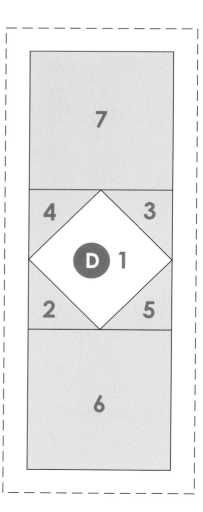

TRADITIONAL PIECING

Numbers on diagram indicate the template number (see chart). See templates on pages 159, 166, 168.

	Cut Qty	Template #
(triangle)	4	24
(rectangle)	2	33
(square)	1	34
(rectangle)	2	35

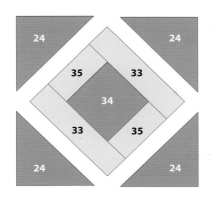

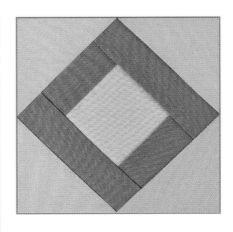

PAPER PIECING

Numbers indicate the piecing order.

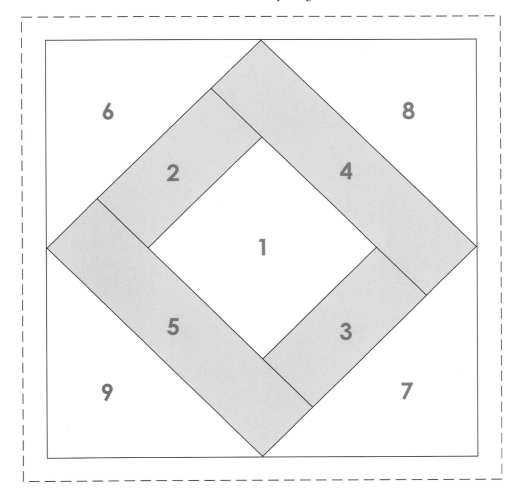

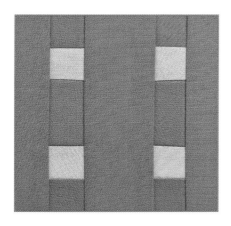

TRADITIONAL PIECING

Numbers on diagram indicate the template number (see chart). See templates on pages 157, 159.

	Cut Qty	Template #
	8	86
	2	81
	2	73
	1	91

PAPER PIECING

Numbers indicate the piecing order.

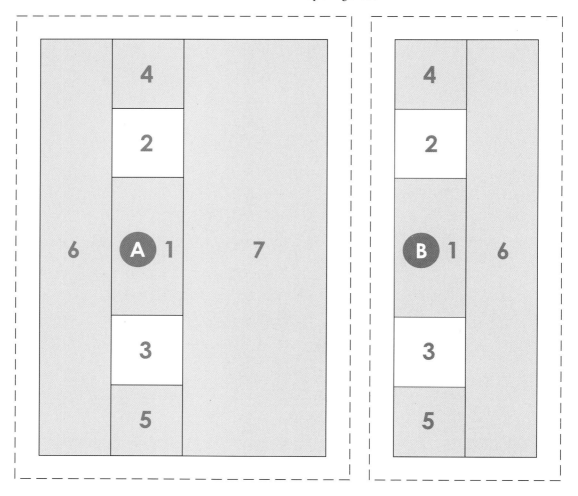

TRADITIONAL PIECING

Numbers on diagram indicate the template number (see chart). See template on page 168.

	Cut Qty	Template #
	8	57

PAPER PIECING

Numbers indicate the piecing order.

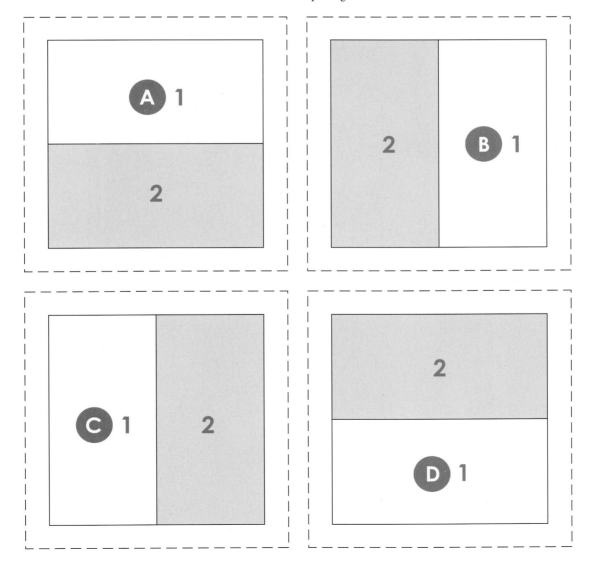

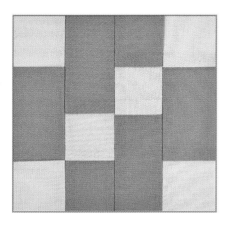

TRADITIONAL PIECING

Numbers on diagram indicate the template number (see chart). See templates on pages 157, 168.

	Cut Qty	Template #
	4	57
	8	61

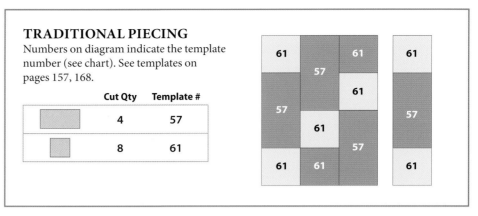

PAPER PIECING

Numbers indicate the piecing order.

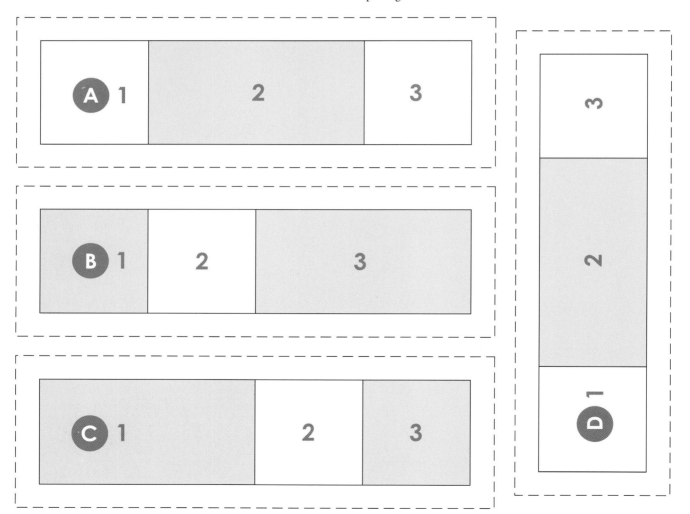

TRADITIONAL PIECING

Numbers on diagram indicate the template number (see chart). See template on page 157.

	Cut Qty	Template #
▨	36	86

PAPER PIECING

Numbers indicate the piecing order.

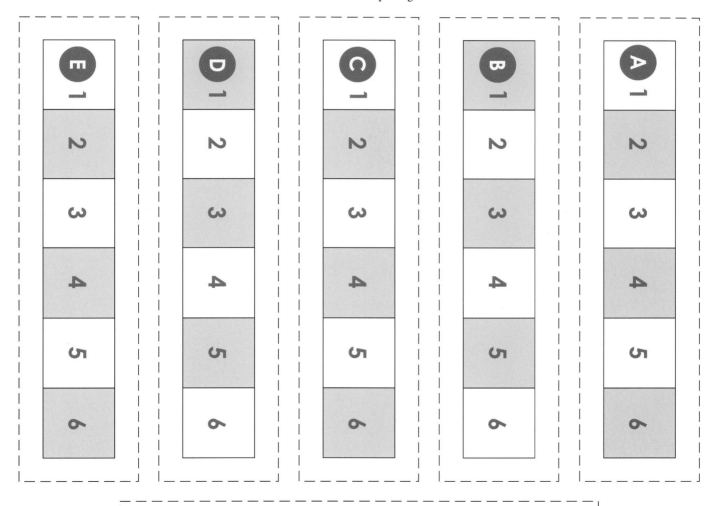

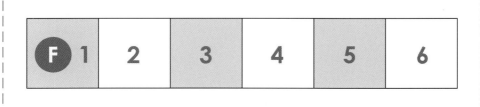

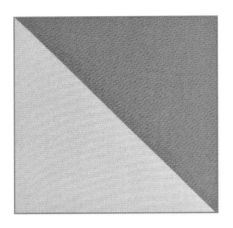

TRADITIONAL PIECING

Numbers on diagram indicate the template number (see chart). See template on page 165.

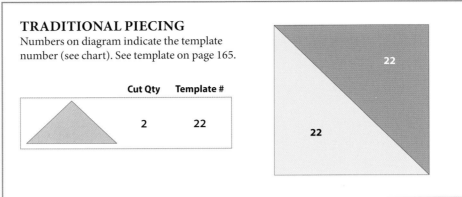

	Cut Qty	Template #
	2	22

PAPER PIECING

Numbers indicate the piecing order.

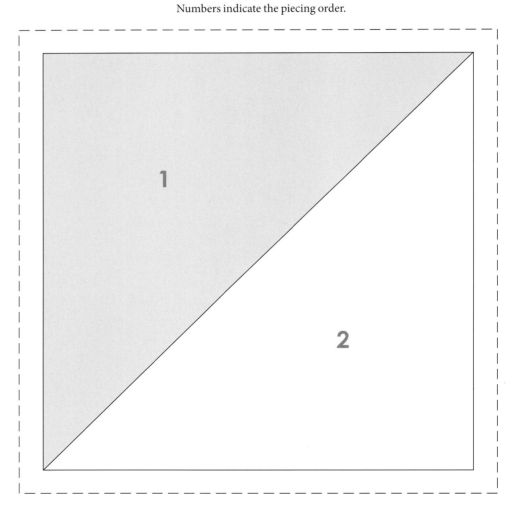

TRADITIONAL PIECING

Numbers on diagram indicate the template number (see chart). See templates on pages 159, 168.

	Cut Qty	Template #
	6	3
	6	4
	1	62

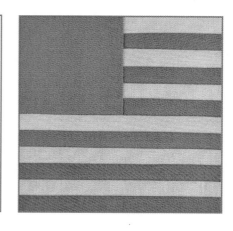

PAPER PIECING

Numbers indicate the piecing order.

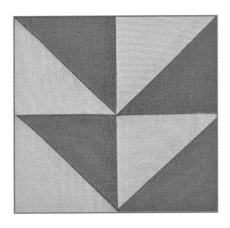

TRADITIONAL PIECING

Numbers on diagram indicate the template number (see chart). See template on page 166.

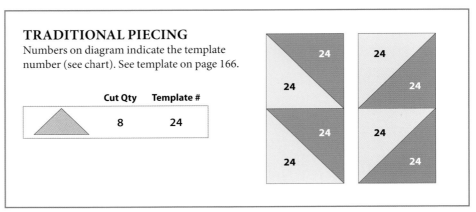

	Cut Qty	Template #
	8	24

PAPER PIECING
Numbers indicate the piecing order.

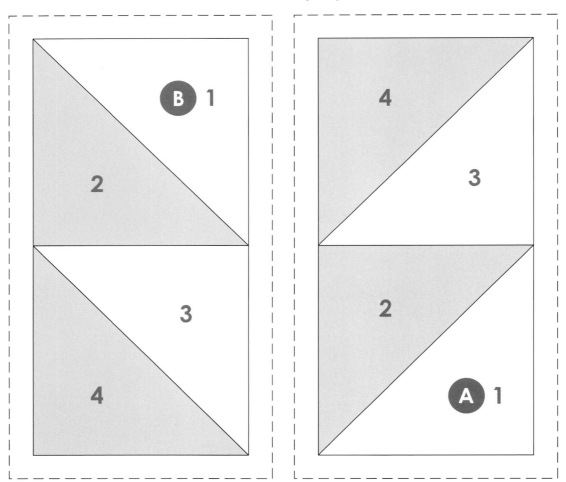

TRADITIONAL PIECING

Numbers on diagram indicate the template number (see chart). See templates on page 166.

	Cut Qty	Template #
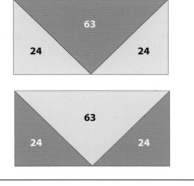	4	24
	2	63

PAPER PIECING

Numbers indicate the piecing order.

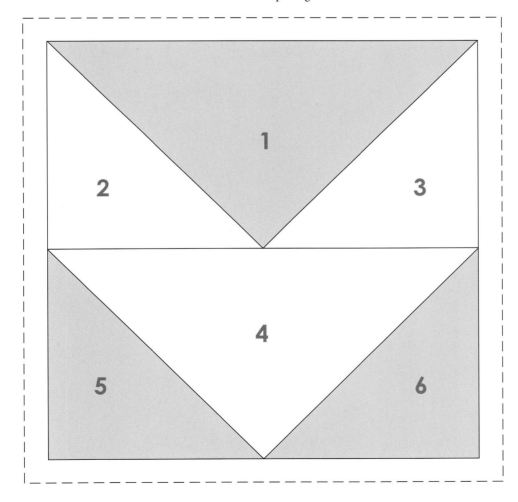

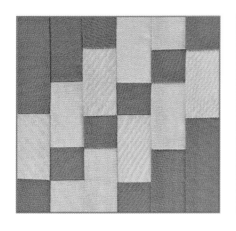

TRADITIONAL PIECING

Numbers on diagram indicate the template number (see chart). See templates on pages 157, 159, 168.

	Cut Qty	Template #
	10	86
	10	81
	2	88

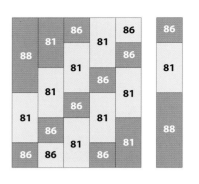

PAPER PIECING

Numbers indicate the piecing order.

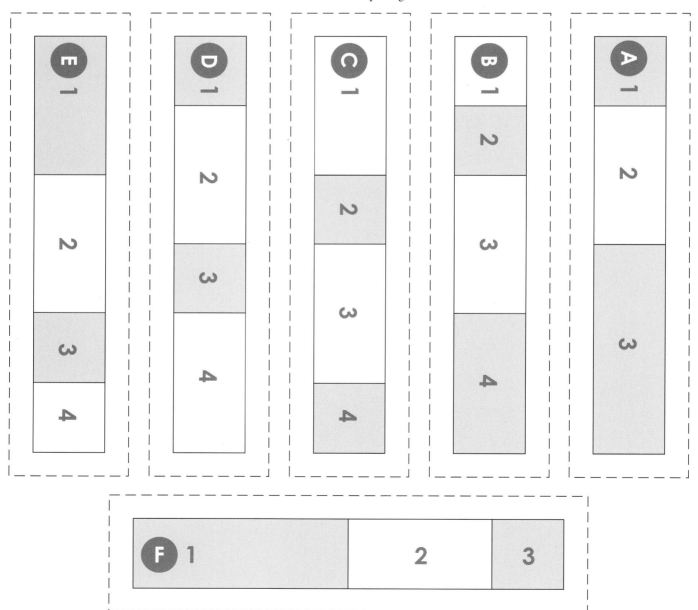

TRADITIONAL PIECING

Numbers on diagram indicate the template number (see chart). See templates on pages 160, 165.

	Cut Qty	Template #
triangle	8	5
hexagon	4	32

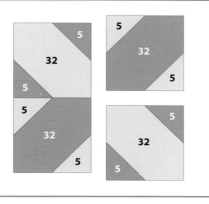

PAPER PIECING

Numbers indicate the piecing order.

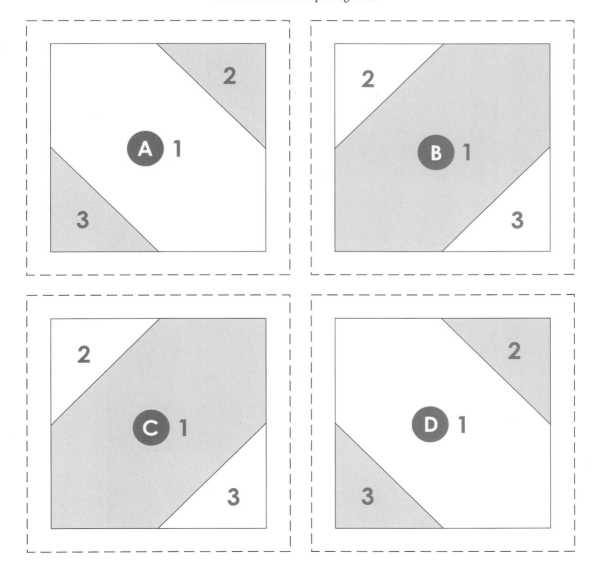

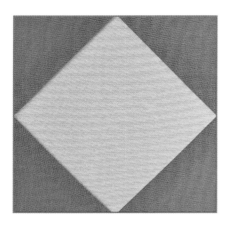

TRADITIONAL PIECING

Numbers on diagram indicate the template number (see chart). See templates on pages 159, 166.

	Cut Qty	Template #
△	4	24
◻	1	58

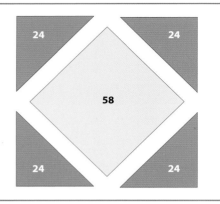

PAPER PIECING

Numbers indicate the piecing order.

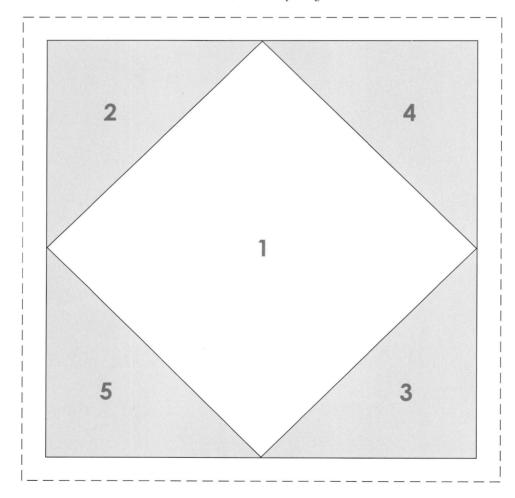

TRADITIONAL PIECING

Numbers on diagram indicate the template number (see chart). See templates on pages 159, 168.

	Cut Qty	Template #
	5	43
	2	72

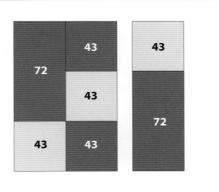

PAPER PIECING

Numbers indicate the piecing order.

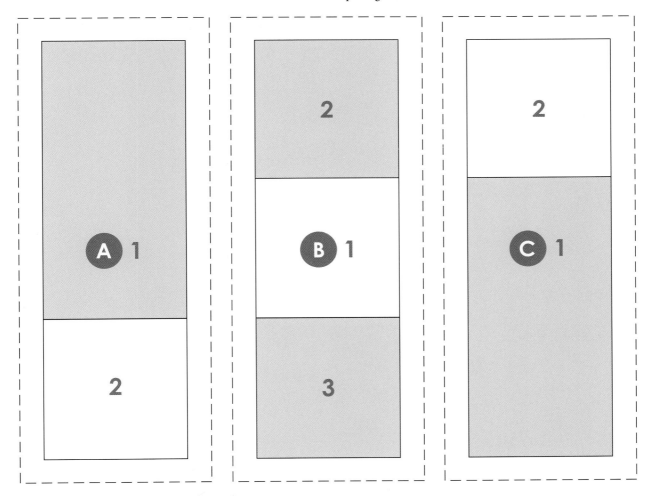

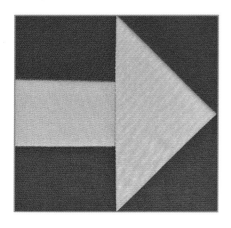

TRADITIONAL PIECING

Numbers on diagram indicate the template number (see chart). See templates on pages 158, 166.

	Cut Qty	Template #
▲	2	24
▲	1	63
▭	3	110

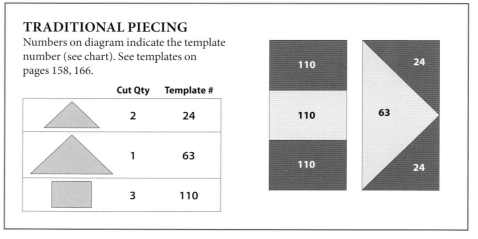

PAPER PIECING

Numbers indicate the piecing order.

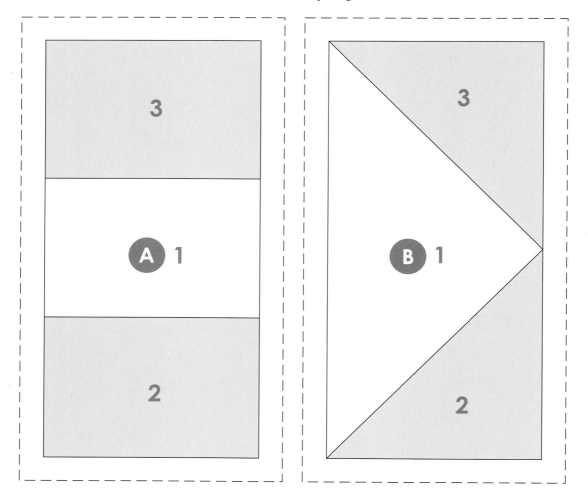

TRADITIONAL PIECING

Numbers on diagram indicate the template number (see chart). See templates on pages 159–60, 167.

	Cut Qty	Template #
▲	12	5
▲	6	28
■	2	31

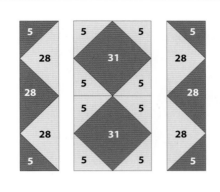

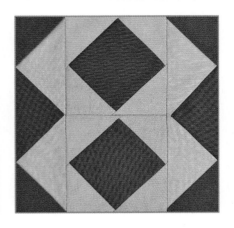

PAPER PIECING
Numbers indicate the piecing order.

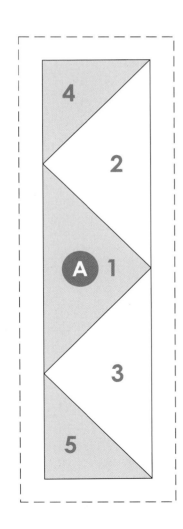

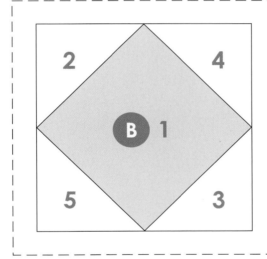

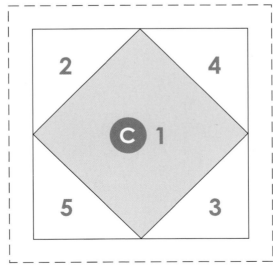

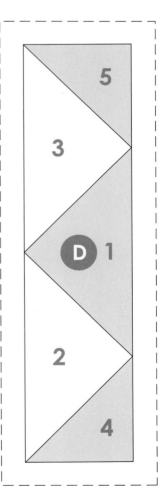

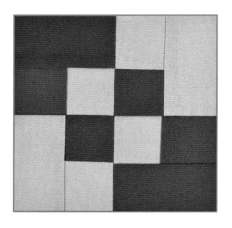

TRADITIONAL PIECING

Numbers on diagram indicate the template number (see chart). See templates on pages 157, 168.

	Cut Qty	Template #
	4	57
	8	61

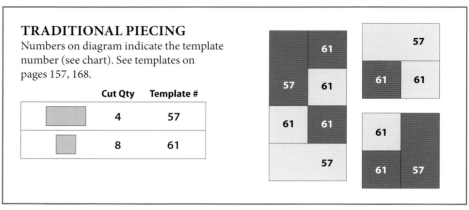

PAPER PIECING

Numbers indicate the piecing order.

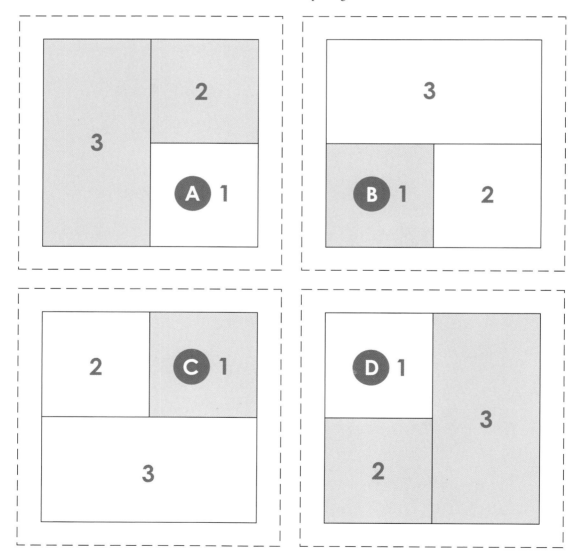

TRADITIONAL PIECING

Numbers on diagram indicate the template number (see chart). See templates on pages 163–64, 167.

	Cut Qty	Template #
	8	101
	8	100
	4	102

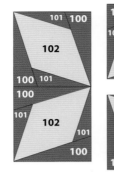
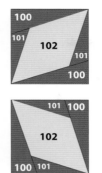
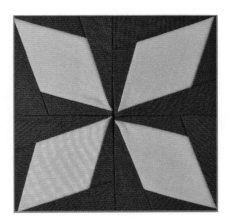

PAPER PIECING
Numbers indicate the piecing order.

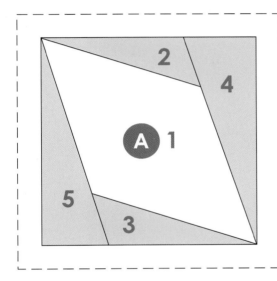
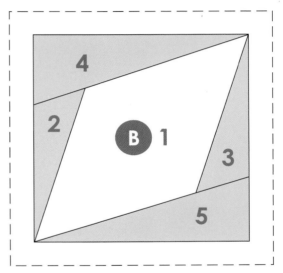
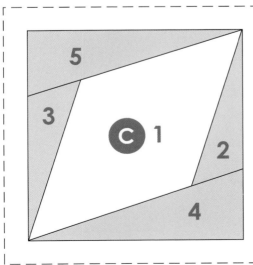
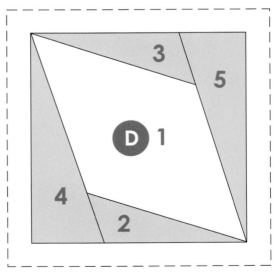

TRADITIONAL PIECING

Numbers on diagram indicate the template number (see chart). See templates on pages 160–61.

	Cut Qty	Template #
▲	2	5
▱	2	6
▱	2	7
▱	2	8

PAPER PIECING

Numbers indicate the piecing order.

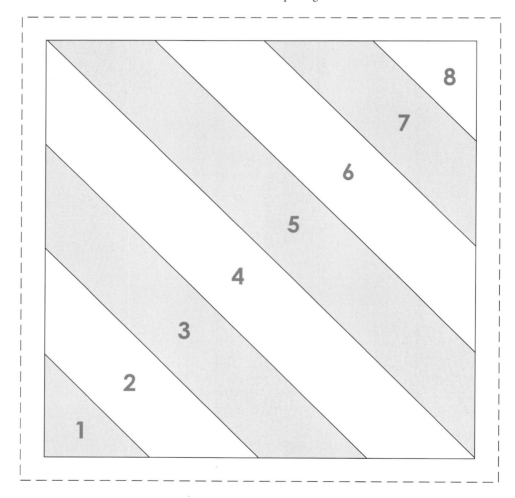

TRADITIONAL PIECING

Numbers on diagram indicate the template number (see chart). See templates on pages 157, 159, 168, 171.

	Cut Qty	Template #
	8	86
	2	81
	2	88
	2	89
	2	90

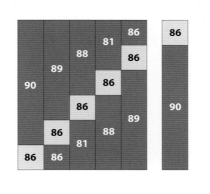

PAPER PIECING

Numbers indicate the piecing order.

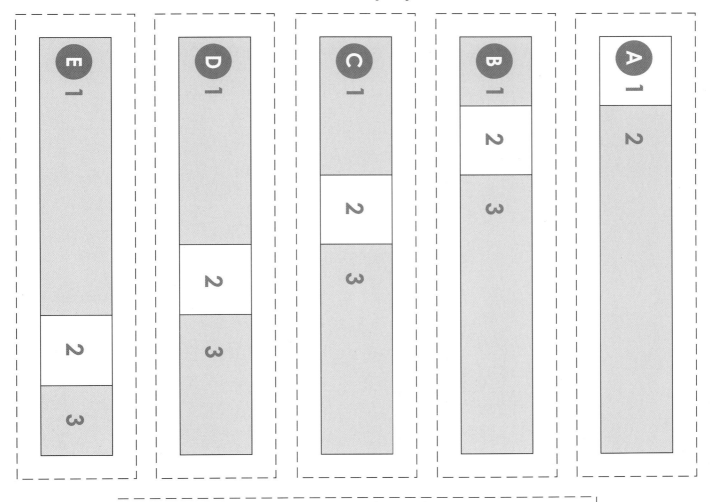

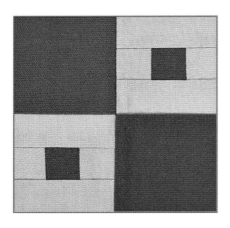

TRADITIONAL PIECING

Numbers on diagram indicate the template number (see chart). See templates on pages 157, 168.

	Cut Qty	Template #
	6	86
	4	88
	2	62

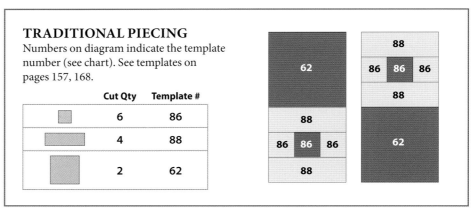

PAPER PIECING

Numbers indicate the piecing order.

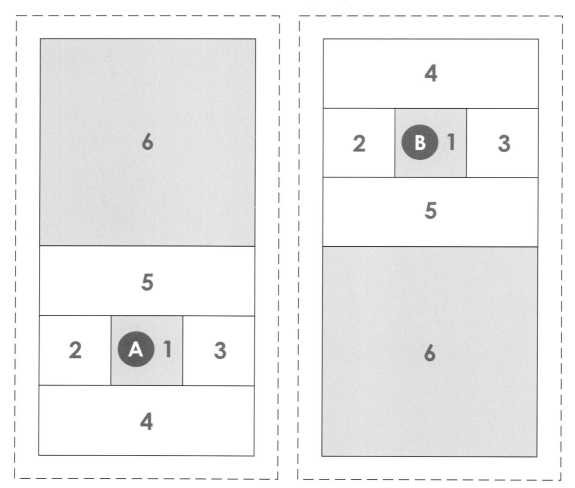

TRADITIONAL PIECING

Numbers on diagram indicate the template number (see chart). See templates on pages 161–63.

	Cut Qty	Template #
	2	9
	2	10
	2	11
	2	12
	2	13
	2	14
	2	15
	2	16

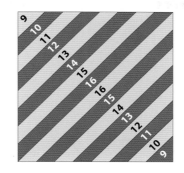

PAPER PIECING

Numbers indicate the piecing order.

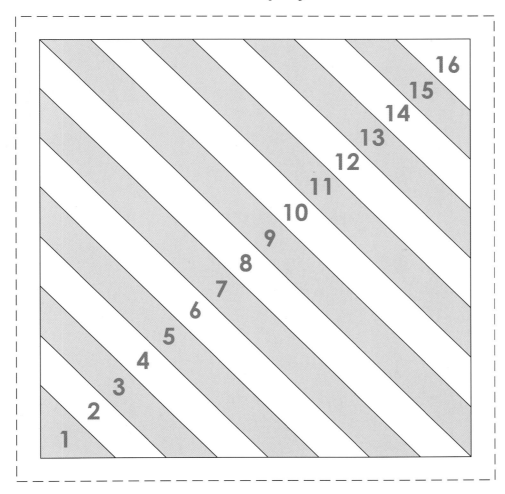

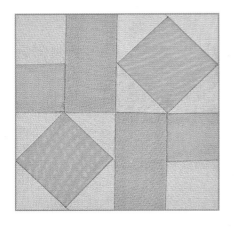

TRADITIONAL PIECING

Numbers on diagram indicate the template number (see chart). See templates on pages 157, 159–60, 168.

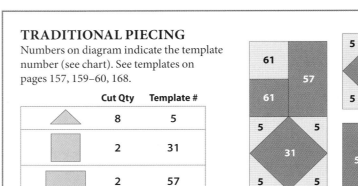

	Cut Qty	Template #
▱	8	5
▢	2	31
▭	2	57
▪	4	61

PAPER PIECING

Numbers indicate the piecing order.

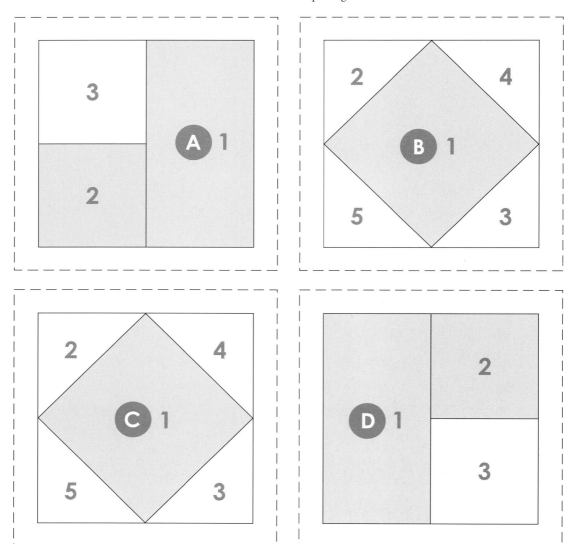

TRADITIONAL PIECING

Numbers on diagram indicate the template number (see chart). See templates on pages 159, 164, 168.

	Cut Qty	Template #
▲	4	129
▽	4	132
▽	4	131
▽	4	130
▢	1	58

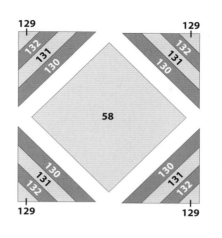

PAPER PIECING

Numbers indicate the piecing order.

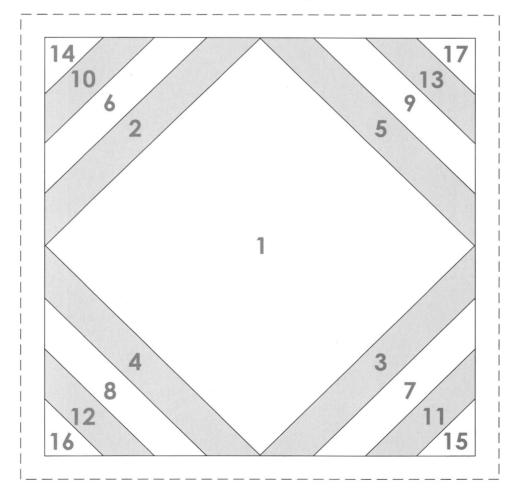

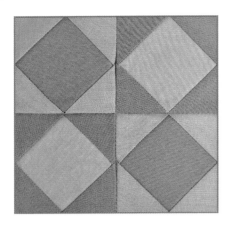

TRADITIONAL PIECING

Numbers on diagram indicate the template number (see chart). See templates on pages 159–60.

	Cut Qty	Template #
△	16	5
▢	4	31

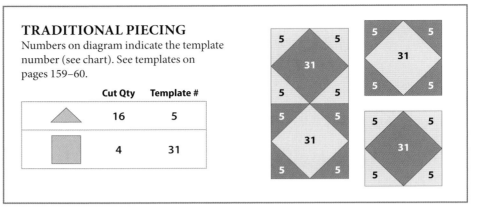

PAPER PIECING

Numbers indicate the piecing order.

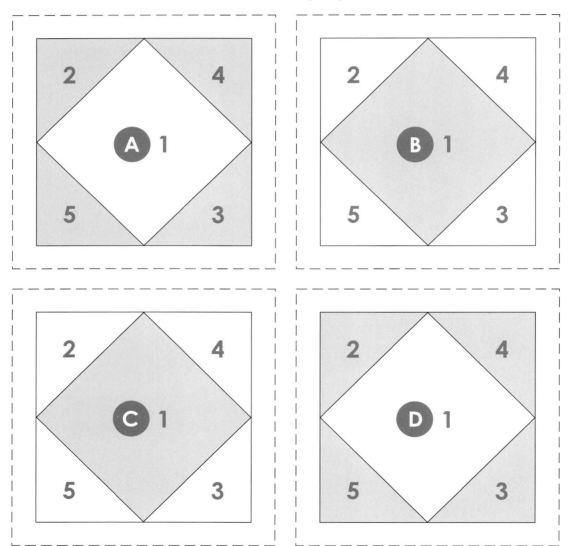

TRADITIONAL PIECING

Numbers on diagram indicate the template number (see chart). See templates on pages 160, 166.

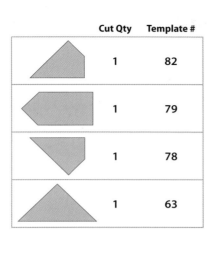

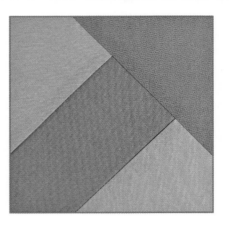

	Cut Qty	Template #
	1	82
	1	79
	1	78
	1	63

PAPER PIECING

Numbers indicate the piecing order.

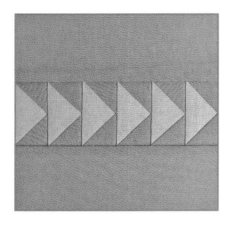

TRADITIONAL PIECING

Numbers on diagram indicate the template number (see chart). See templates on pages 157, 164, 166.

	Cut Qty	Template #
△	12	44
△	6	76
▭	2	56

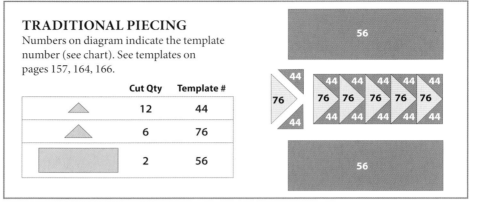

PAPER PIECING

Numbers indicate the piecing order.

TRADITIONAL PIECING

Numbers on diagram indicate the template number (see chart). See templates on pages 157, 160, 166.

	Cut Qty	Template #
	2	73
	6	74
	3	70

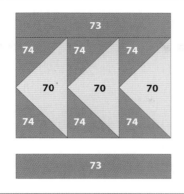

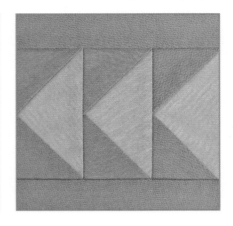

PAPER PIECING

Numbers indicate the piecing order.

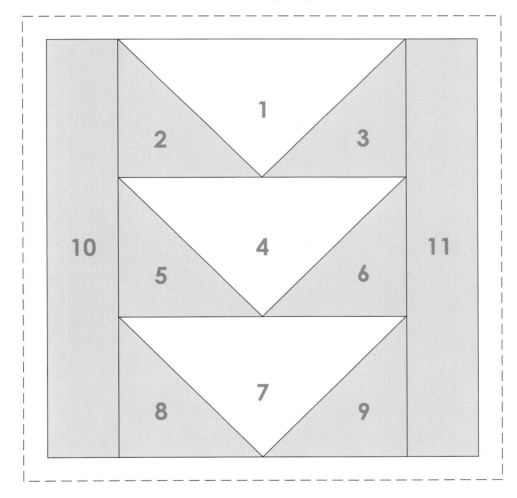

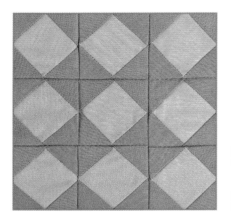

TRADITIONAL PIECING

Numbers on diagram indicate the template number (see chart). See templates on pages 157, 164.

	Cut Qty	Template #
◣	36	44
◆	9	45

PAPER PIECING

Numbers indicate the piecing order.

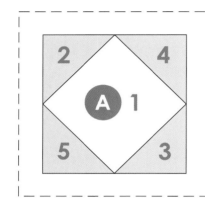 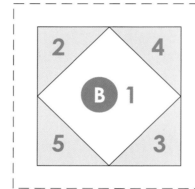 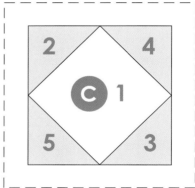

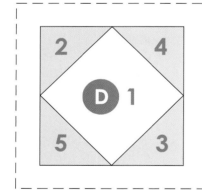 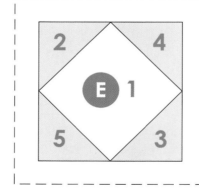 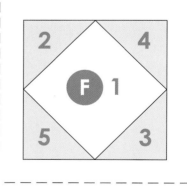

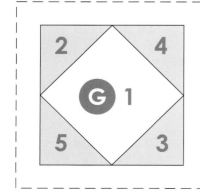 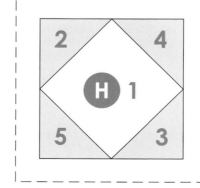 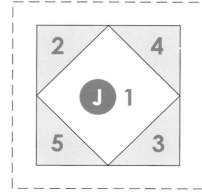

TRADITIONAL PIECING

Numbers on diagram indicate the template number (see chart). See templates on pages 164, 168, 170.

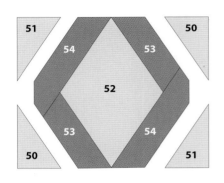

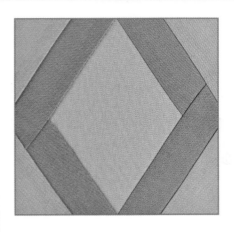

	Cut Qty	Template #
	2	50
	2	51
	1	52
	2	53
	2	54

PAPER PIECING

Numbers indicate the piecing order.

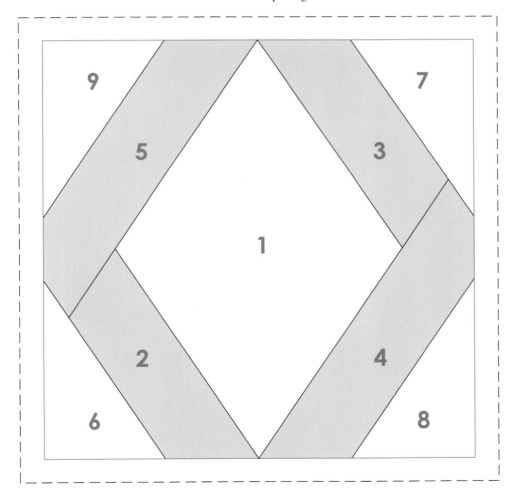

TRADITIONAL PIECING

Numbers on diagram indicate the template number (see chart). See templates on pages 164, 166.

	Cut Qty	Template #
△	36	44
△	18	76

PAPER PIECING

Numbers indicate the piecing order.

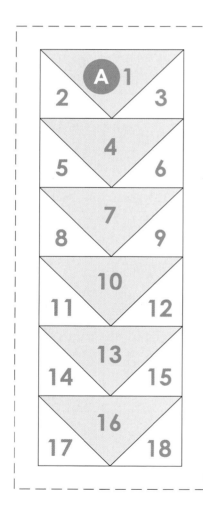

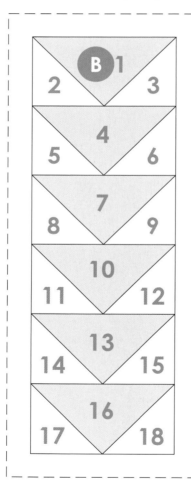

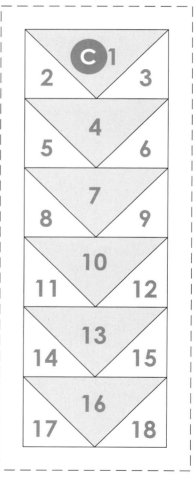

TRADITIONAL PIECING

Numbers on diagram indicate the template number (see chart). See templates on pages 157, 159, 171.

	Cut Qty	Template #
	2	81
	4	89
	2	73
	1	43

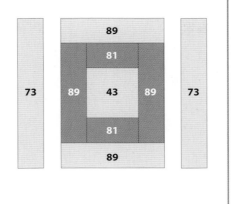

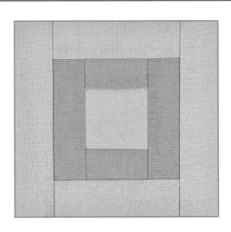

PAPER PIECING

Numbers indicate the piecing order.

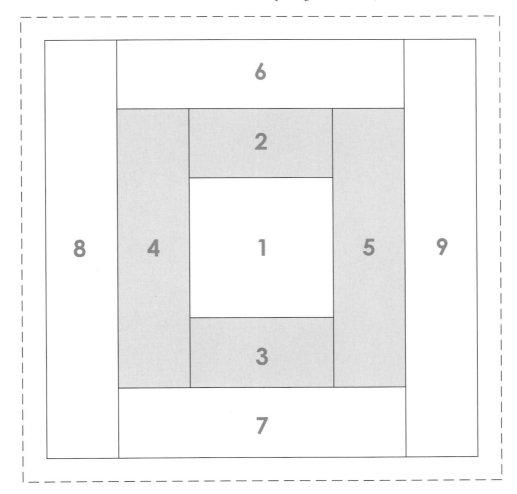

TRADITIONAL PIECING

Numbers on diagram indicate the template number (see chart). See templates on pages 164, 166, 170.

	Cut Qty	Template #
	6	44
	3	76
	15	122
	15	123

PAPER PIECING

Numbers indicate the piecing order.

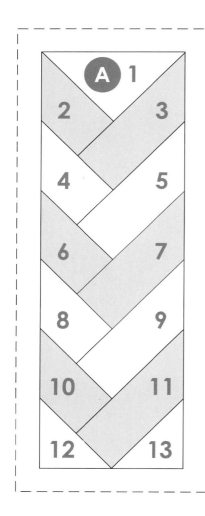
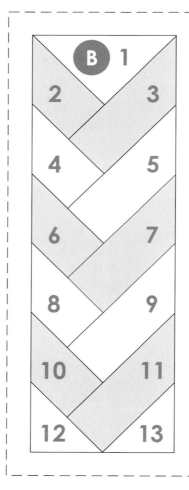
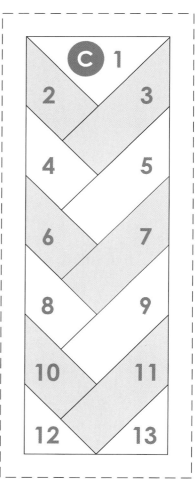

TRADITIONAL PIECING

Numbers on diagram indicate the template number (see chart). See templates on pages 159–60, 167.

	Cut Qty	Template #
▲	12	5
▲	8	28
■	1	31

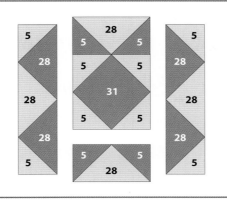

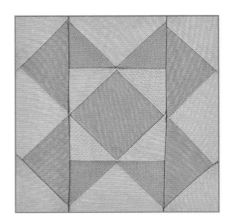

PAPER PIECING

Numbers indicate the piecing order.

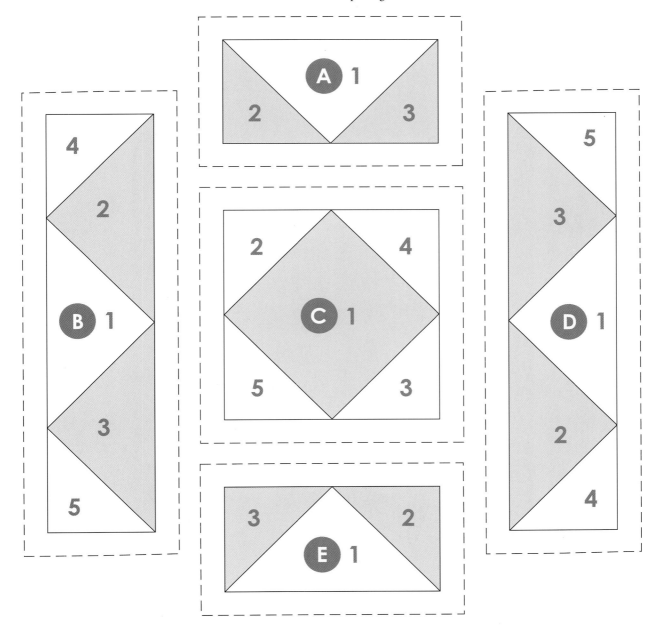

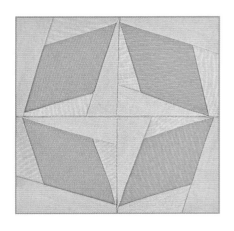

TRADITIONAL PIECING

Numbers on diagram indicate the template number (see chart). See templates on pages 163–64, 167.

	Cut Qty	Template #
	8	101
	8	100
	4	102

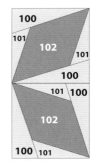
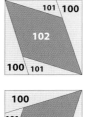

PAPER PIECING

Numbers indicate the piecing order.

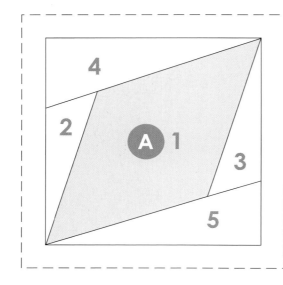
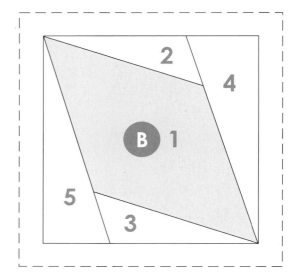
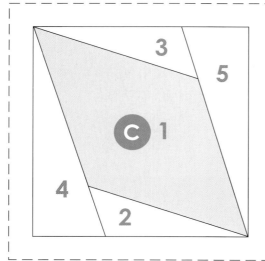
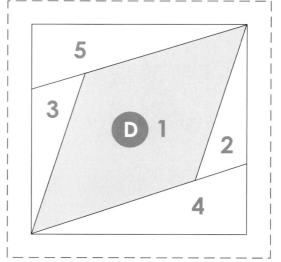

TRADITIONAL PIECING

Numbers on diagram indicate the template number (see chart). See template on page 170.

	Cut Qty	Template #
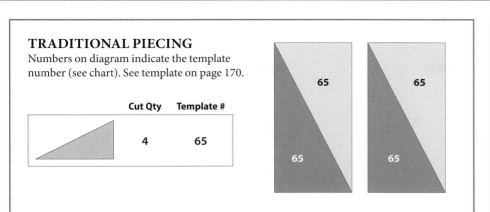	4	65

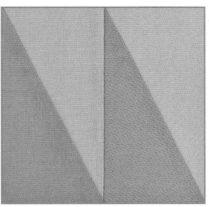

PAPER PIECING

Numbers indicate the piecing order.

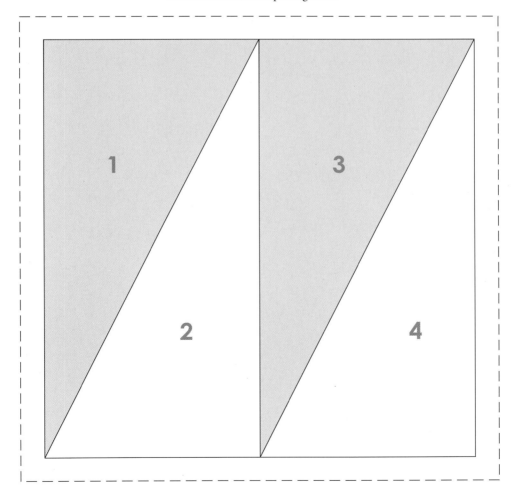

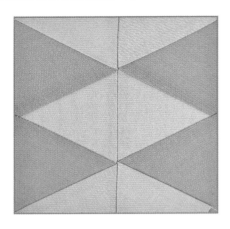

TRADITIONAL PIECING

Numbers on diagram indicate the template number (see chart). See templates on page 168.

	Cut Qty	Template #
	2	47
	6	48
	2	49

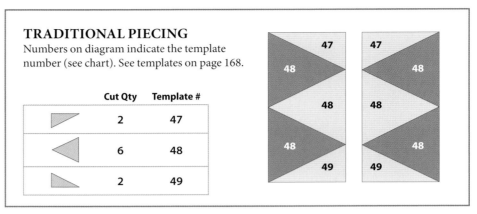

PAPER PIECING

Numbers indicate the piecing order.

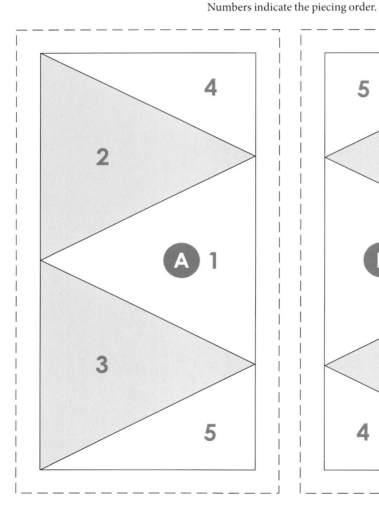

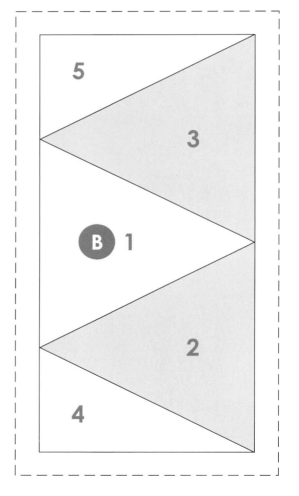

TRADITIONAL PIECING

Numbers on diagram indicate the template number (see chart). See templates on page 166.

	Cut Qty	Template #
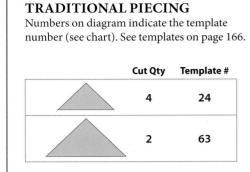	4	24
	2	63

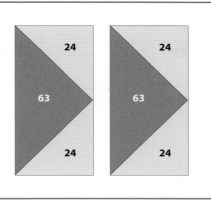

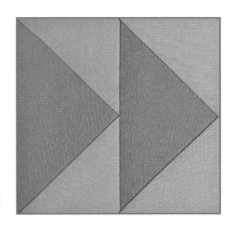

PAPER PIECING

Numbers indicate the piecing order.

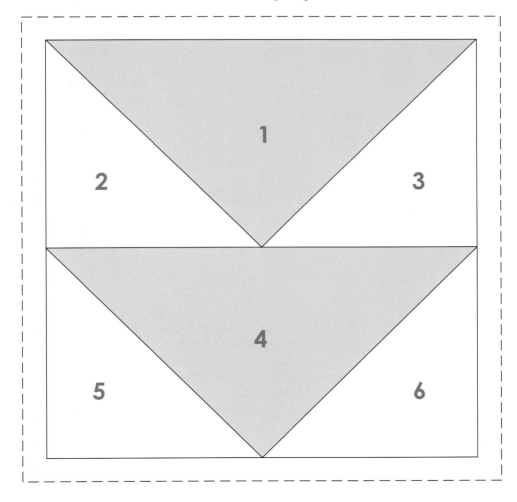

TRADITIONAL PIECING

Numbers on diagram indicate the template number (see chart). See templates on pages 161–63, 165.

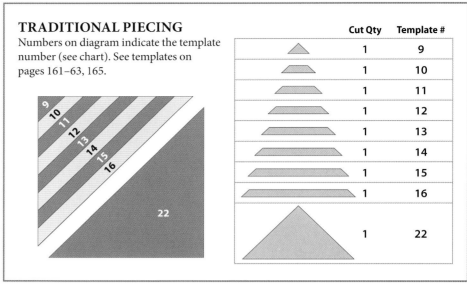

	Cut Qty	Template #
	1	9
	1	10
	1	11
	1	12
	1	13
	1	14
	1	15
	1	16
	1	22

PAPER PIECING

Numbers indicate the piecing order.

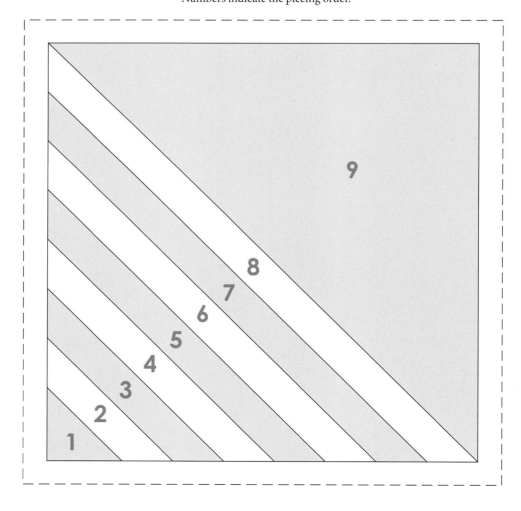

TRADITIONAL PIECING

Numbers on diagram indicate the template number (see chart). See templates on pages 157–58, 160, 164.

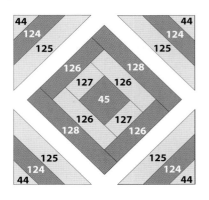

	Cut Qty	Template #
	1	45
	4	124
	4	125
	4	126
	2	127
	2	128
	4	44

PAPER PIECING

Numbers indicate the piecing order.

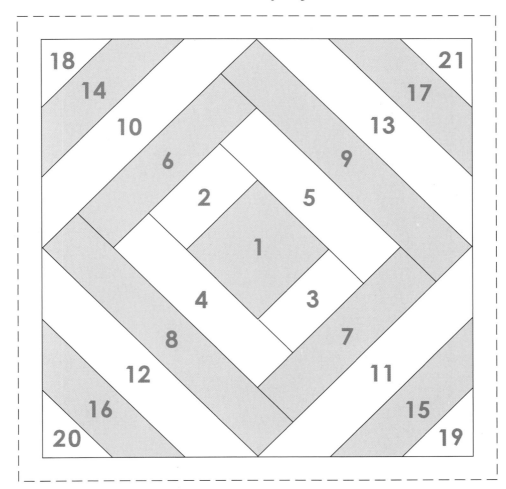

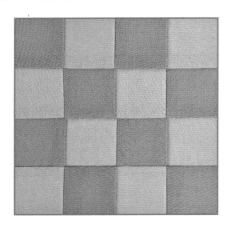

TRADITIONAL PIECING

Numbers on diagram indicate the template number (see chart). See template on page 157.

	Cut Qty	Template #
	16	61

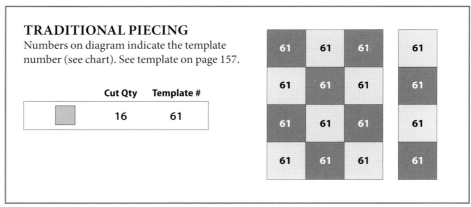

PAPER PIECING

Numbers indicate the piecing order.

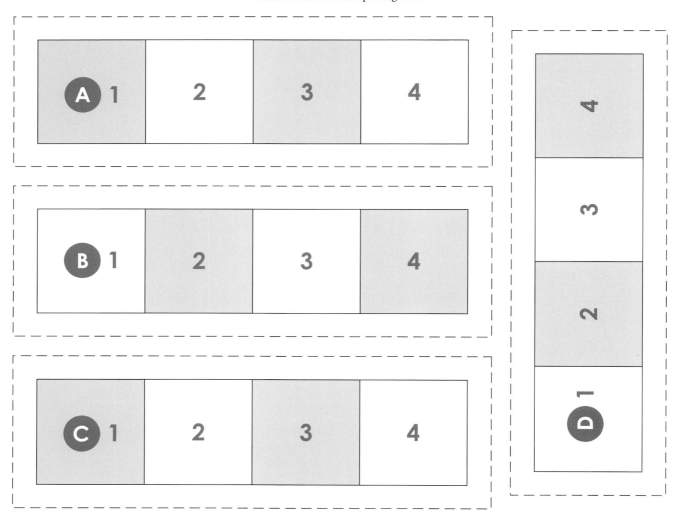

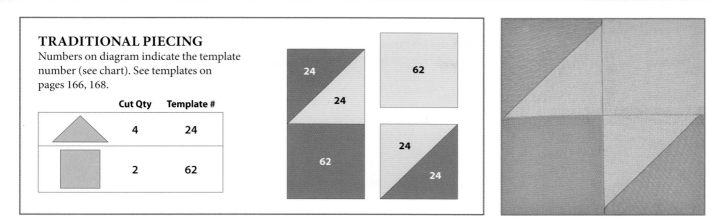

TRADITIONAL PIECING

Numbers on diagram indicate the template number (see chart). See templates on pages 166, 168.

	Cut Qty	Template #
▲	4	24
■	2	62

PAPER PIECING

Numbers indicate the piecing order.

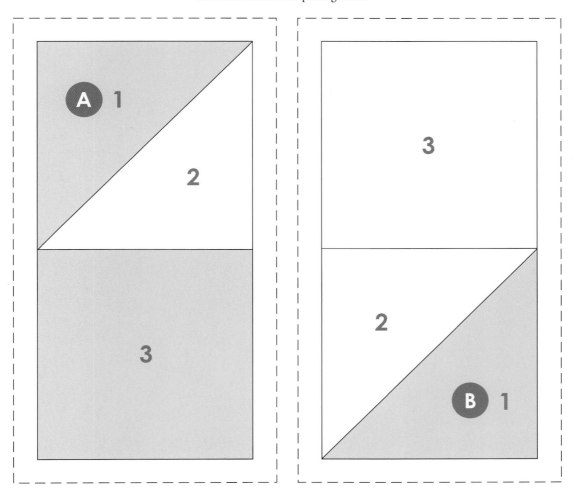

TRADITIONAL PIECING

Numbers on diagram indicate the template number (see chart). See templates on page 167.

	Cut Qty	Template #
▲	2	133
▱	2	138
⬡	1	118

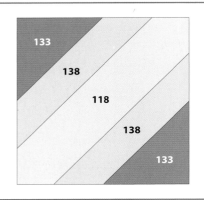

PAPER PIECING

Numbers indicate the piecing order.

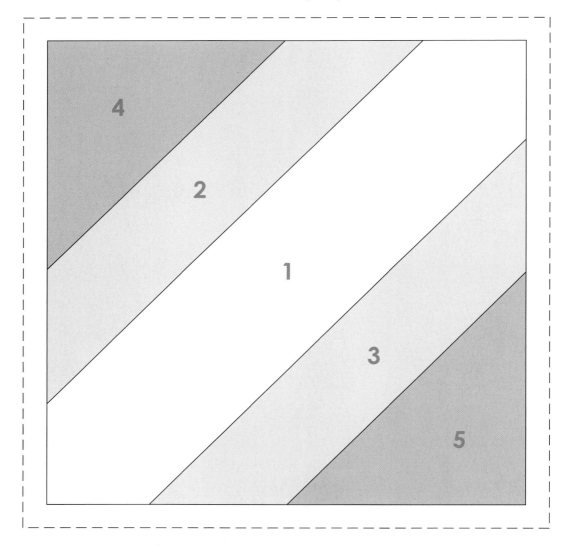

TRADITIONAL PIECING

Numbers on diagram indicate the template number (see chart). See templates on pages 157, 160, 166.

	Cut Qty	Template #
	6	74
	3	70
	1	56

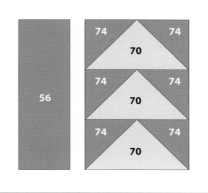

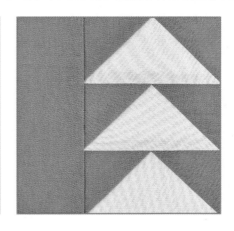

PAPER PIECING

Numbers indicate the piecing order.

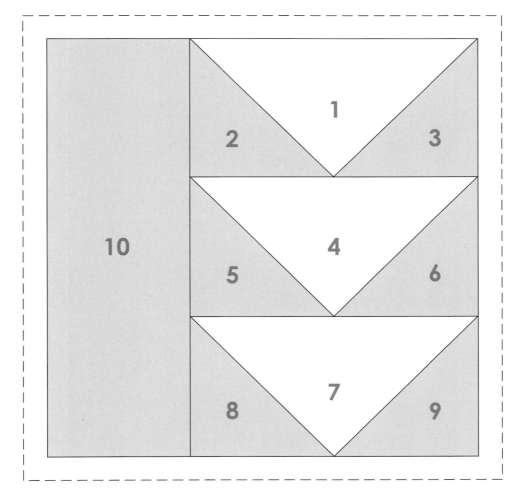

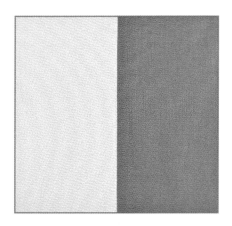

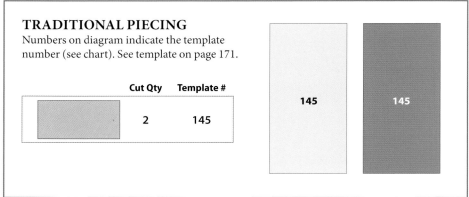

TRADITIONAL PIECING

Numbers on diagram indicate the template number (see chart). See template on page 171.

	Cut Qty	Template #
	2	145

PAPER PIECING

Numbers indicate the piecing order.

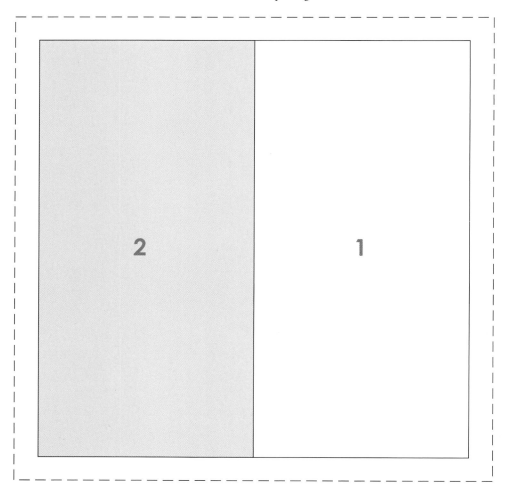

TRADITIONAL PIECING

Numbers on diagram indicate the template number (see chart). See templates on pages 163, 165–66.

	Cut Qty	Template #
	1	24
	1	23
	1	22

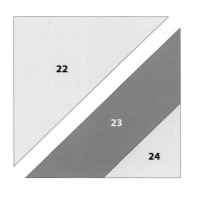

PAPER PIECING

Numbers indicate the piecing order.

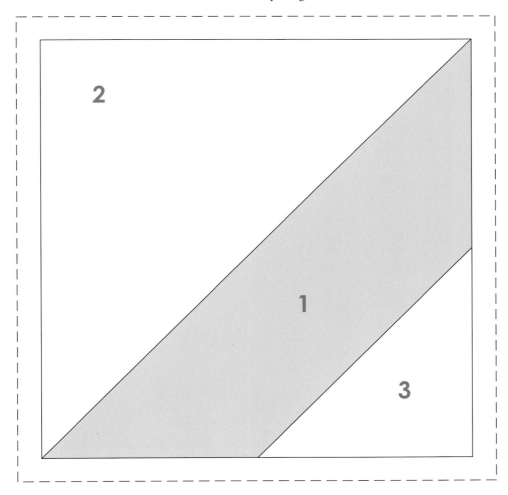

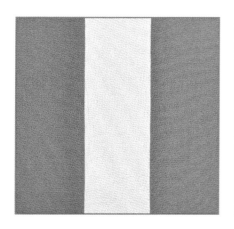

TRADITIONAL PIECING

Numbers on diagram indicate the template number (see chart). See template on page 157.

	Cut Qty	Template #
	3	56

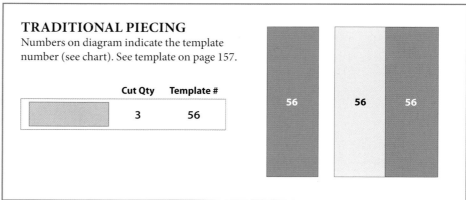

PAPER PIECING

Numbers indicate the piecing order.

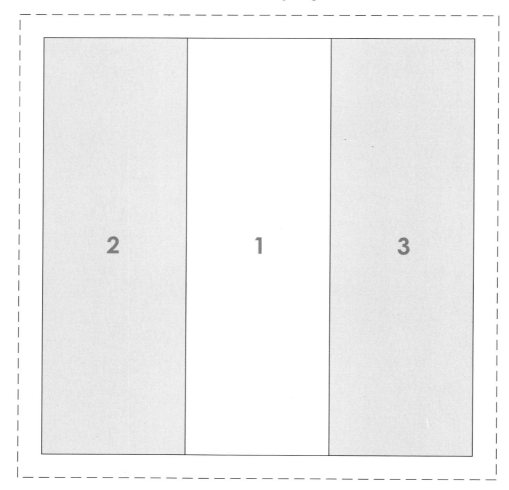

TRADITIONAL PIECING

Numbers on diagram indicate the template number (see chart). See templates on pages 160–61, 163–64, 172.

	Cut Qty	Template #
	4	9
	2	17
	2	18
	2	155
	2	156
	4	5
	4	6

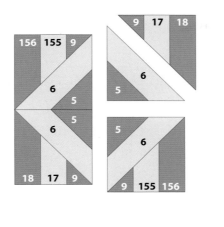

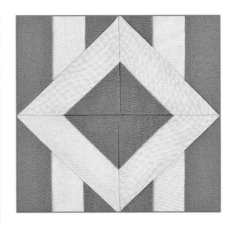

PAPER PIECING

Numbers indicate the piecing order.

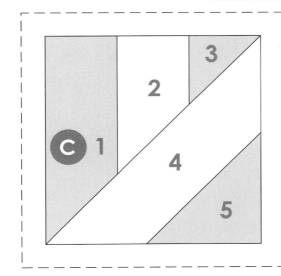

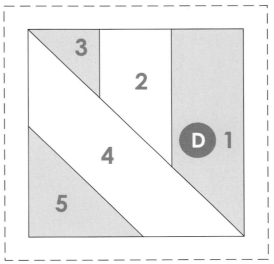

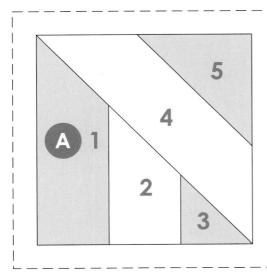

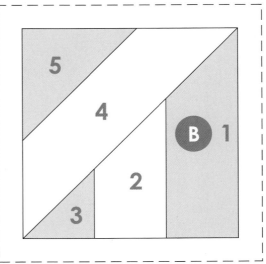

TRADITIONAL PIECING

Numbers on diagram indicate the template number (see chart). See templates on page 170.

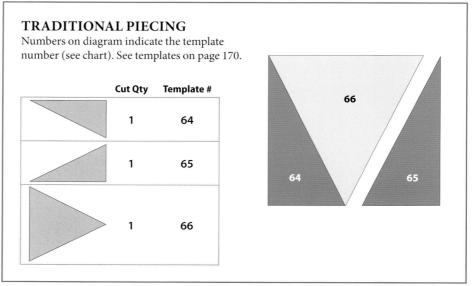

	Cut Qty	Template #
	1	64
	1	65
	1	66

PAPER PIECING

Numbers indicate the piecing order.

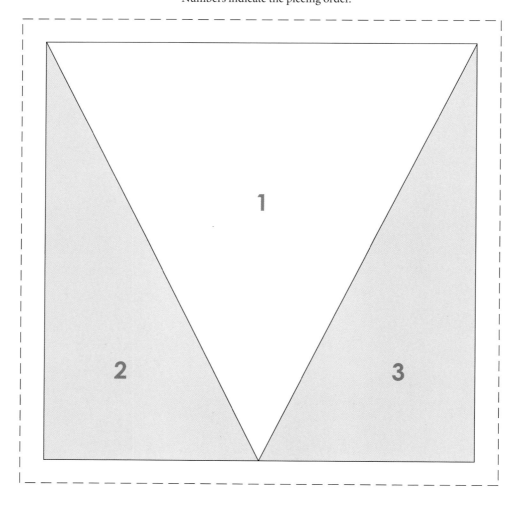

TRADITIONAL PIECING

Numbers on diagram indicate the template number (see chart). See templates on pages 157, 168, 171.

	Cut Qty	Template #
	4	89
	2	73
	1	72

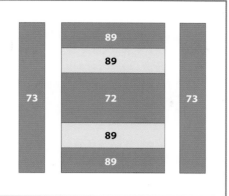

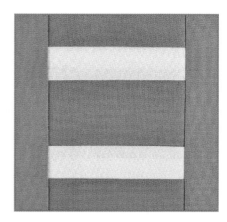

PAPER PIECING

Numbers indicate the piecing order.

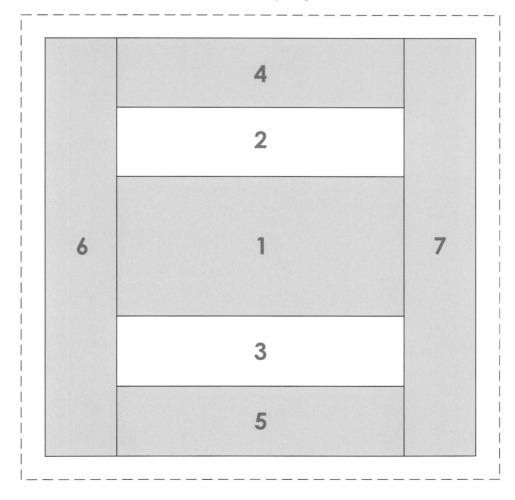

TRADITIONAL PIECING

Numbers on diagram indicate the template number (see chart). See template on page 159.

	Cut Qty	Template #
	9	43

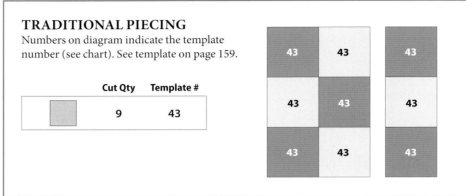

PAPER PIECING

Numbers indicate the piecing order.

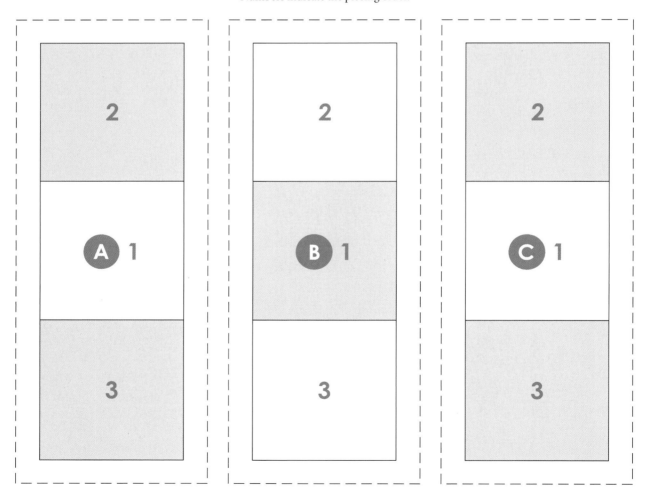

TRADITIONAL PIECING

Numbers on diagram indicate the template number (see chart). See template on page 168.

	Cut Qty	Template #
	4	62

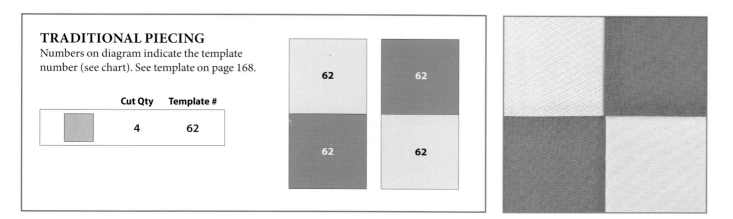

PAPER PIECING

Numbers indicate the piecing order.

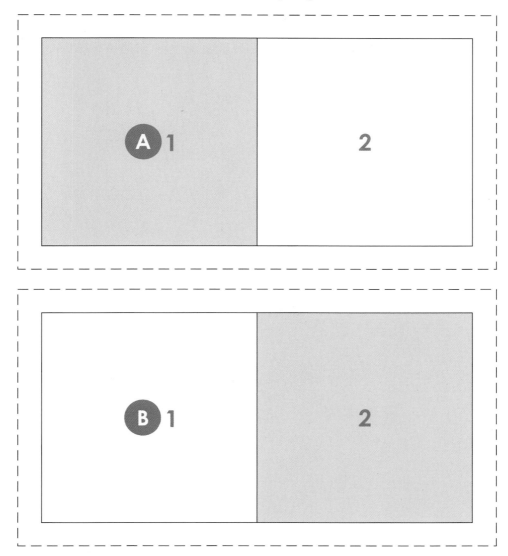

TRADITIONAL PIECING

Numbers on diagram indicate the template number (see chart). See templates on pages 165, 169, 171.

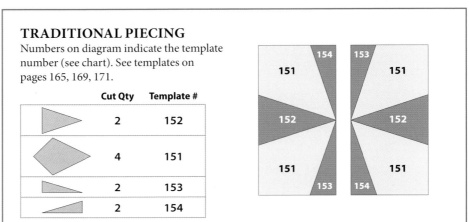

	Cut Qty	Template #
◢	2	152
◆	4	151
◣	2	153
◺	2	154

PAPER PIECING

Numbers indicate the piecing order.

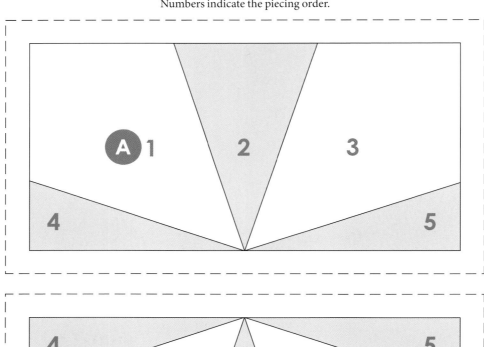

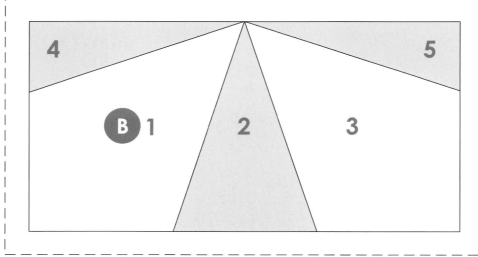

TRADITIONAL PIECING

Numbers on diagram indicate the template number (see chart). See templates on pages 163, 172.

	Cut Qty	Template #
▲	2	9
◢	2	155
◣	2	156
◢	2	157
◢	2	158
◢	2	159

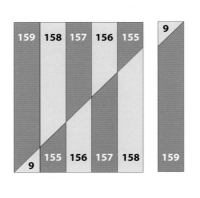

PAPER PIECING
Numbers indicate the piecing order.

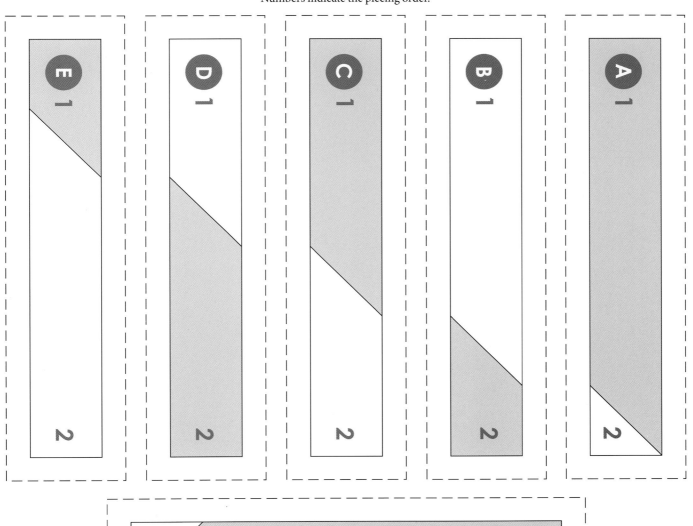

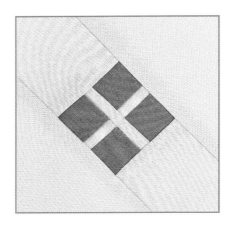

TRADITIONAL PIECING

Numbers on diagram indicate the template number (see chart). See templates on pages 157, 165, 169, 171.

	Cut Qty	Template #
	2	147
	1	150
	4	86
	2	149
	2	148

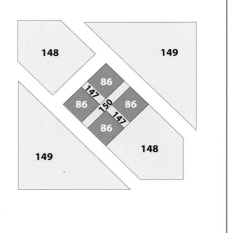

PAPER PIECING

Numbers indicate the piecing order.

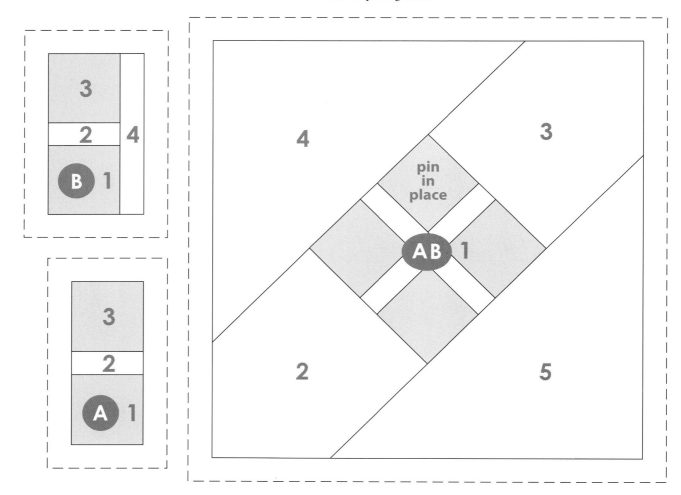

TRADITIONAL PIECING

Numbers on diagram indicate the template number (see chart). See templates on pages 166, 168.

	Cut Qty	Template #
△	4	24
▢	2	62

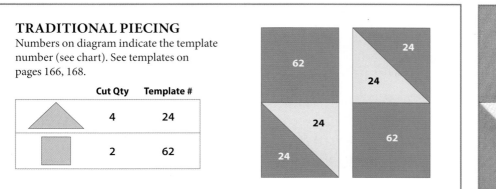

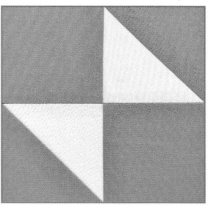

PAPER PIECING

Numbers indicate the piecing order.

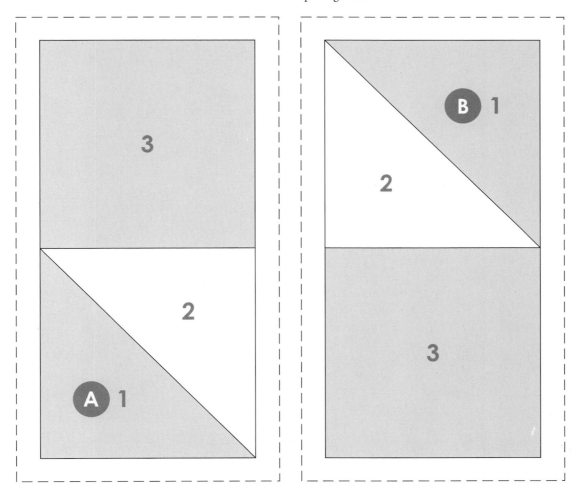

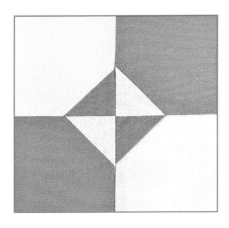

TRADITIONAL PIECING

Numbers on diagram indicate the template number (see chart). See templates on pages 160, 166.

	Cut Qty	Template #
	4	80
	4	5

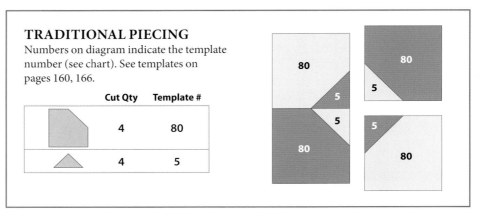

PAPER PIECING

Numbers indicate the piecing order.

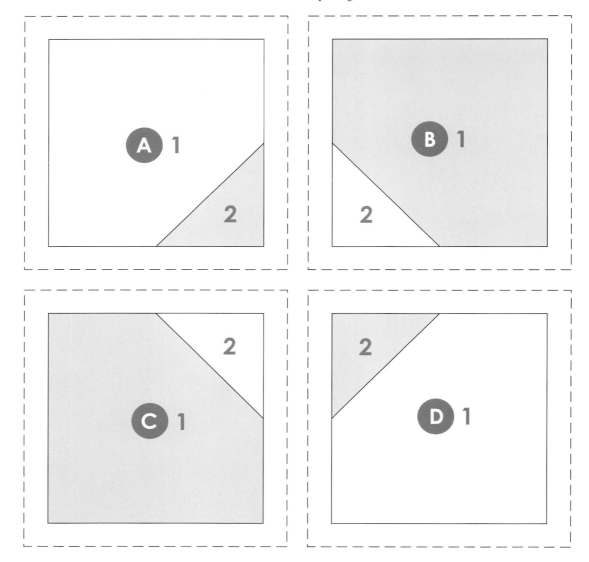

TRADITIONAL PIECING

Numbers on diagram indicate the template number (see chart). See templates on pages 160–61.

	Cut Qty	Template #
▲	8	5
▱	8	6

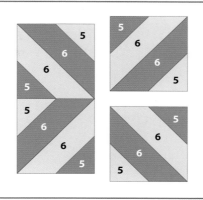

PAPER PIECING
Numbers indicate the piecing order.

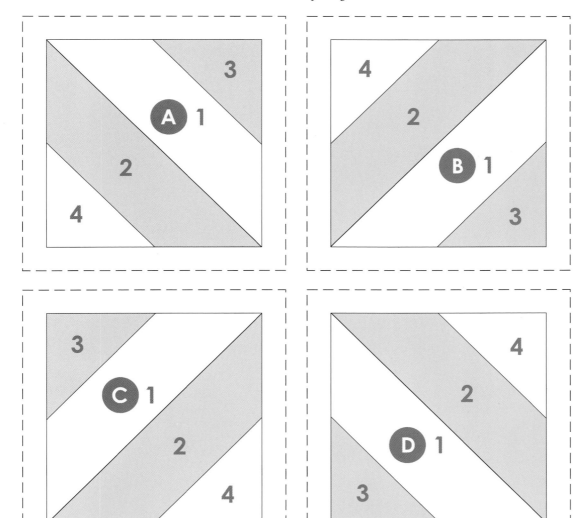

TRADITIONAL PIECING

Numbers on diagram indicate the template number (see chart). See templates on pages 157, 159.

	Cut Qty	Template #
	16	86
	10	81

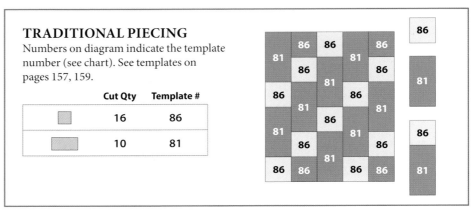

PAPER PIECING

Numbers indicate the piecing order.

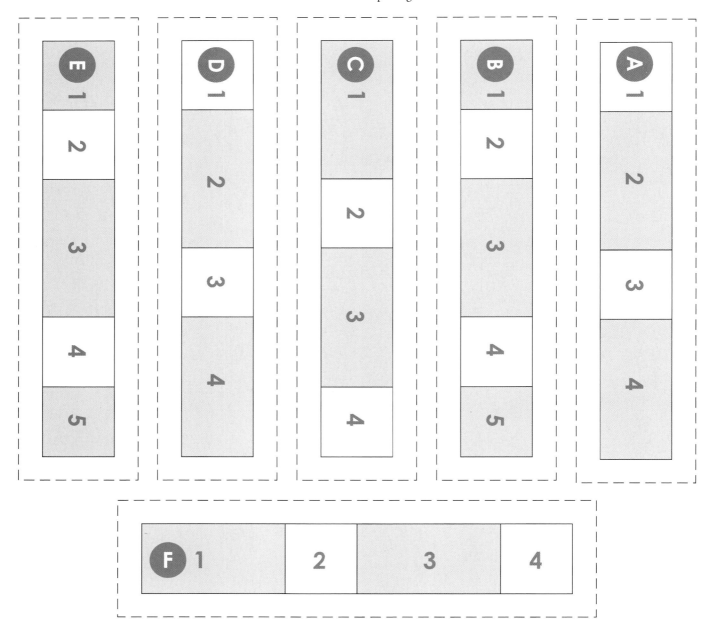

TRADITIONAL PIECING

Numbers on diagram indicate the template number (see chart). See templates on pages 157, 159.

	Cut Qty	Template #
	15	86
	6	1
	2	73
	2	4

PAPER PIECING

Numbers indicate the piecing order.

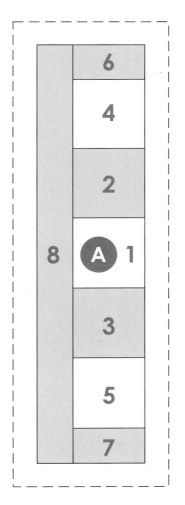

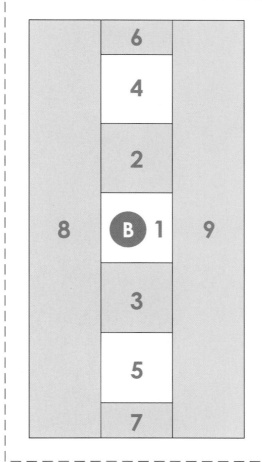

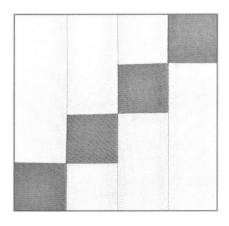

TRADITIONAL PIECING

Numbers on diagram indicate the template number (see chart). See templates on pages 157, 159, 168.

	Cut Qty	Template #
	2	57
	6	61
	2	67

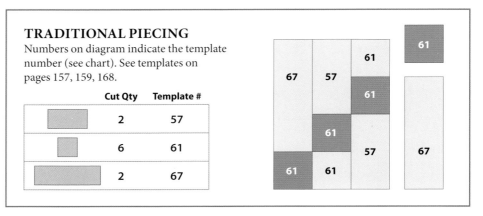

PAPER PIECING

Numbers indicate the piecing order.

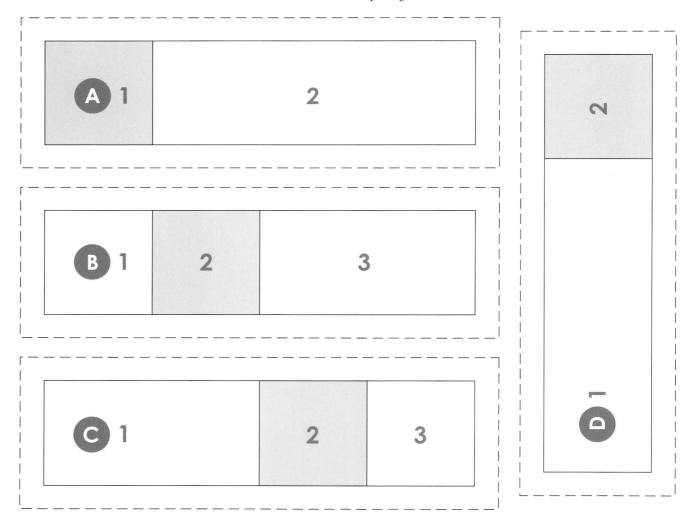

TRADITIONAL PIECING

Numbers on diagram indicate the template number (see chart). See templates on pages 164, 167, 171.

	Cut Qty	Template #
	2	28
	2	29
	2	30
	1	145

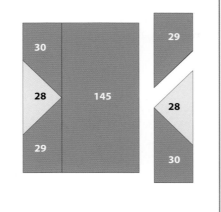

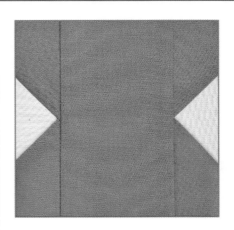

PAPER PIECING

Numbers indicate the piecing order.

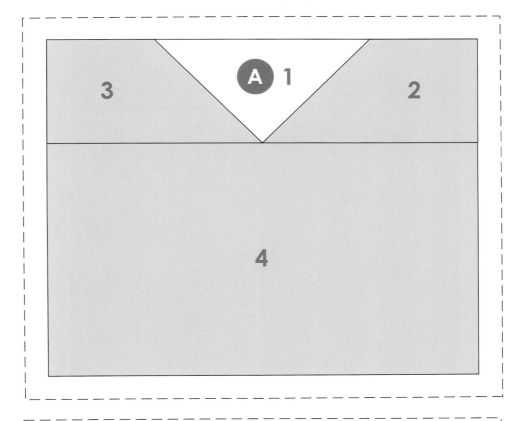

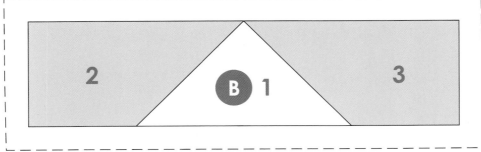

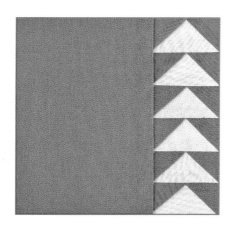

TRADITIONAL PIECING

Numbers on diagram indicate the template number (see chart). See templates on pages 164, 166, 171.

	Cut Qty	Template #
▲	12	44
▲	6	76
▭	1	146

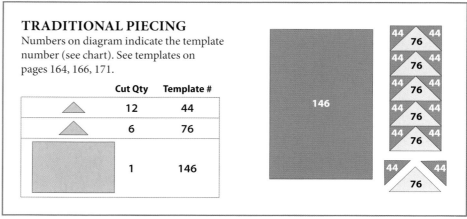

PAPER PIECING

Numbers indicate the piecing order.

TRADITIONAL PIECING

Numbers on diagram indicate the template number (see chart). See templates on pages 163, 165, 172.

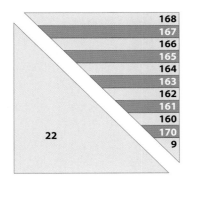

	Cut Qty	Template #
	1	9
	1	170
	1	160
	1	161
	1	162
	1	163
	1	164
	1	165
	1	166
	1	167
	1	168
	1	22

PAPER PIECING

Numbers indicate the piecing order.

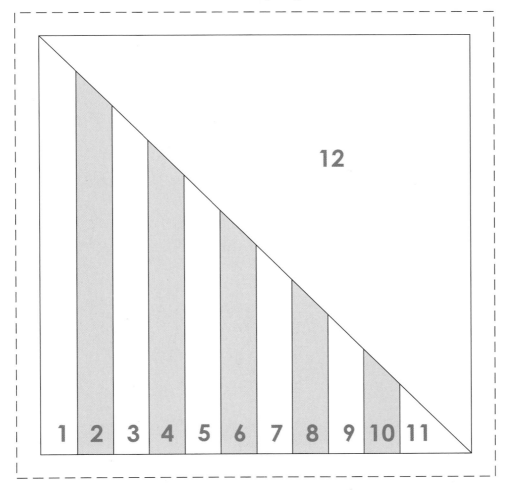

TRADITIONAL PIECING

Numbers on diagram indicate the template number (see chart). See templates on pages 160, 166.

	Cut Qty	Template #
	2	83
	2	84
	2	85
	4	24

PAPER PIECING

Numbers indicate the piecing order.

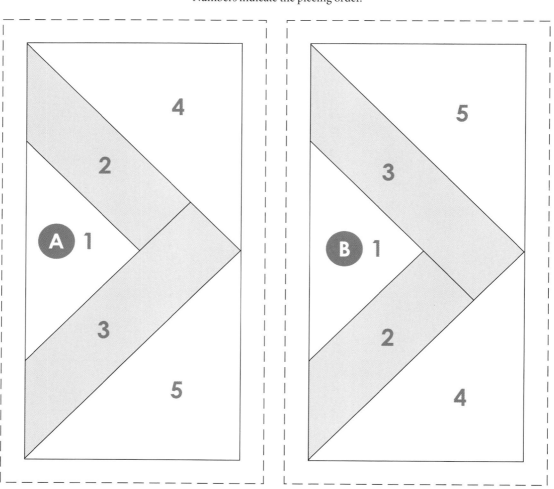

Traditional Piecing Templates

When piecing traditionally, follow the same numerical order on the diagram that you do for the paper piecing. Ensure you use a ¼" (6mm) seam allowance and press after joining each piece.

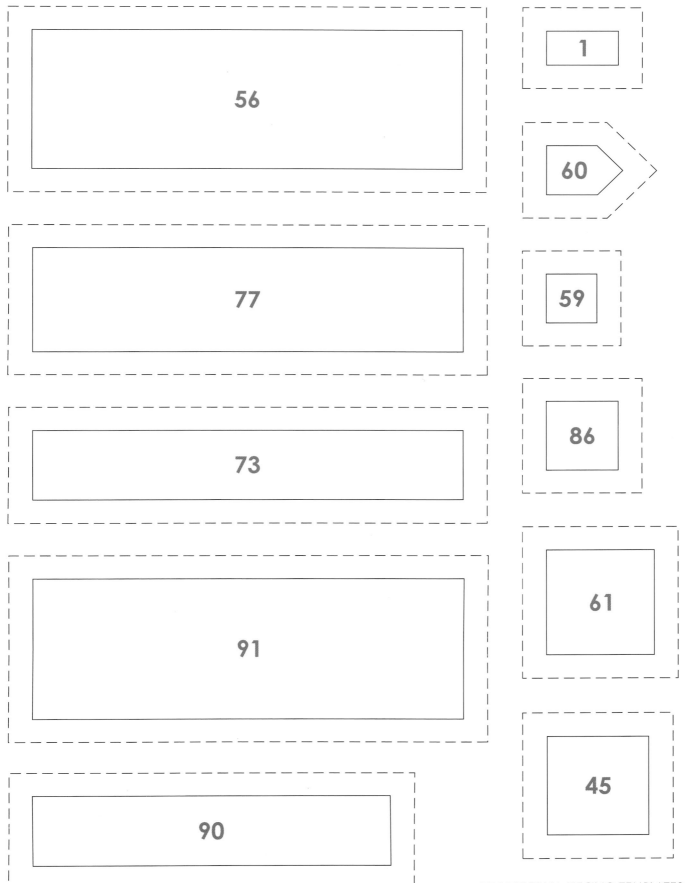

56

1

60

77

59

73

86

91

61

90

45

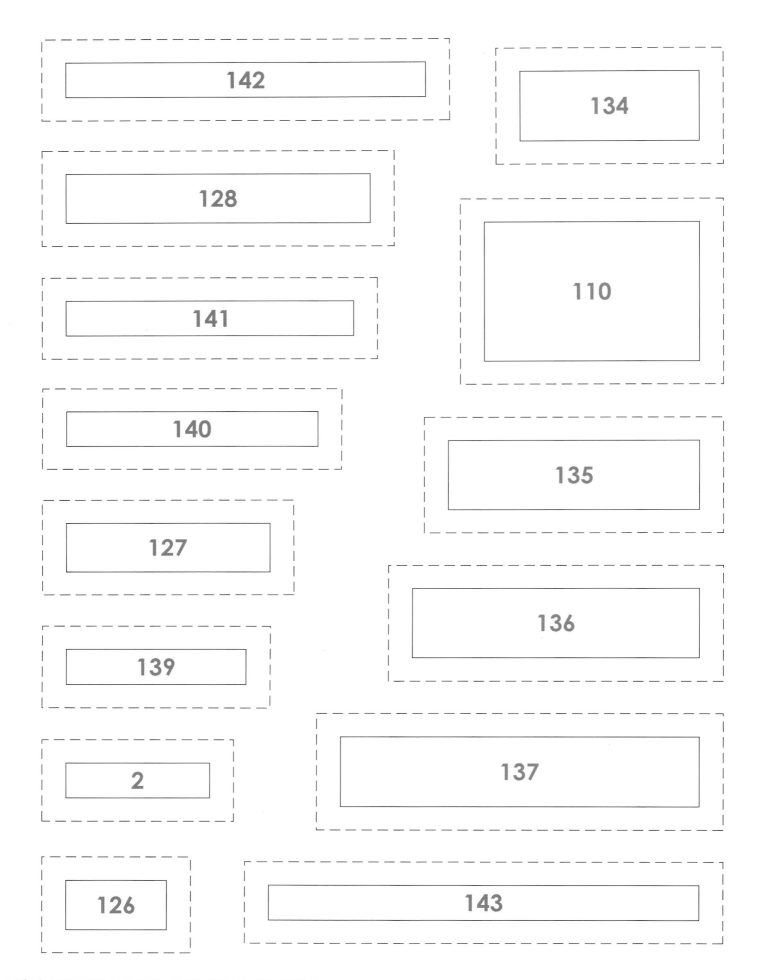

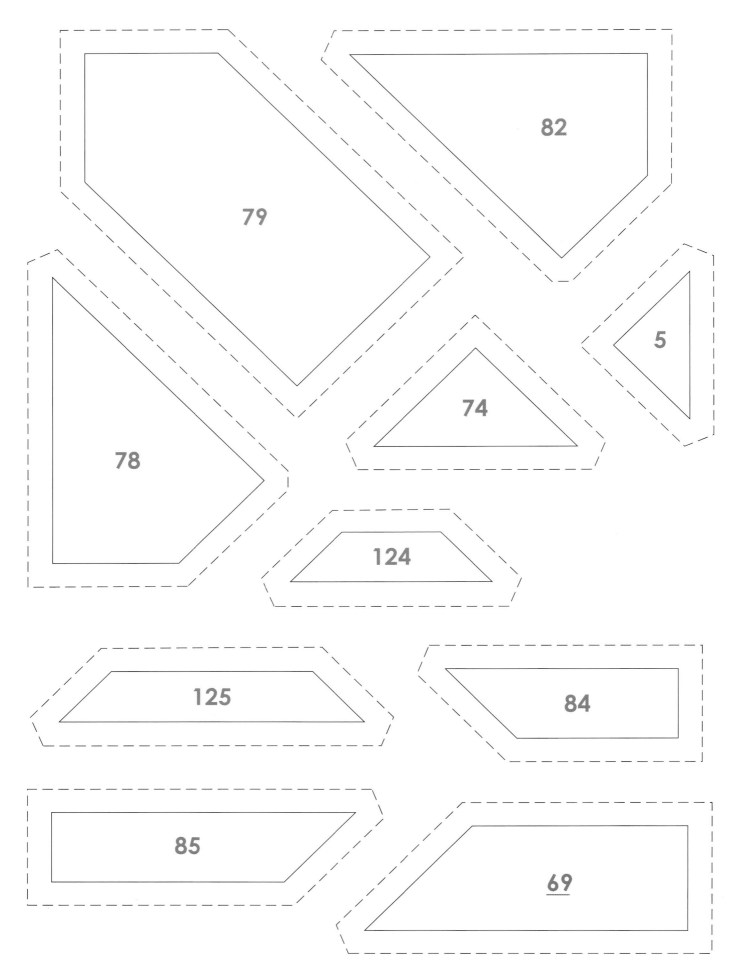

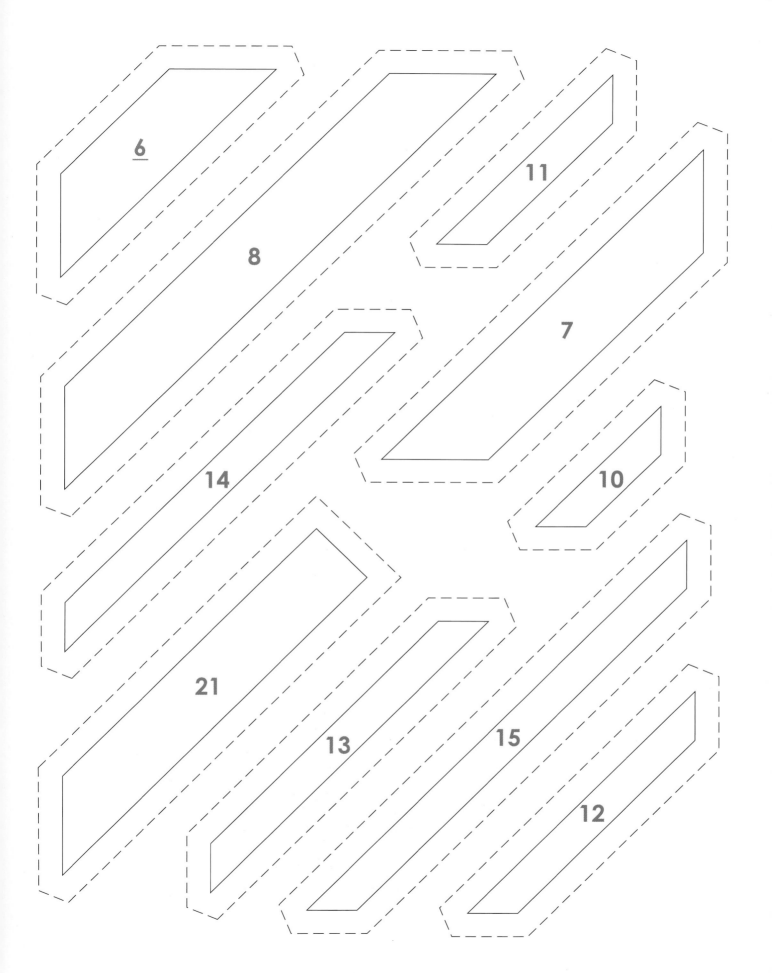

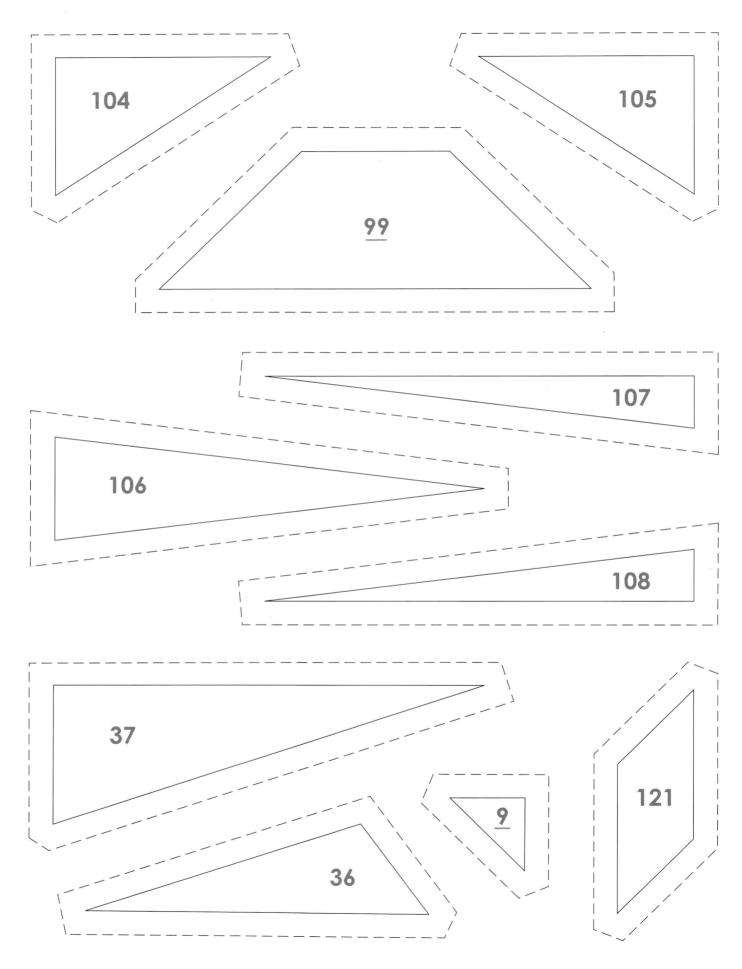

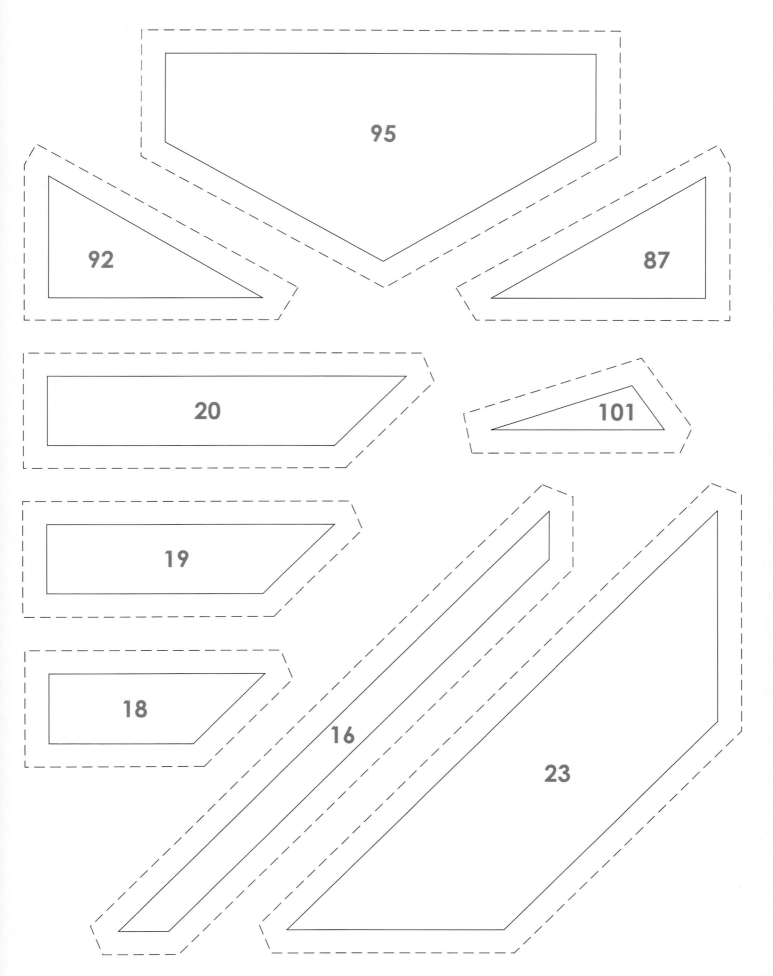

95

92

87

20

101

19

16

18

23

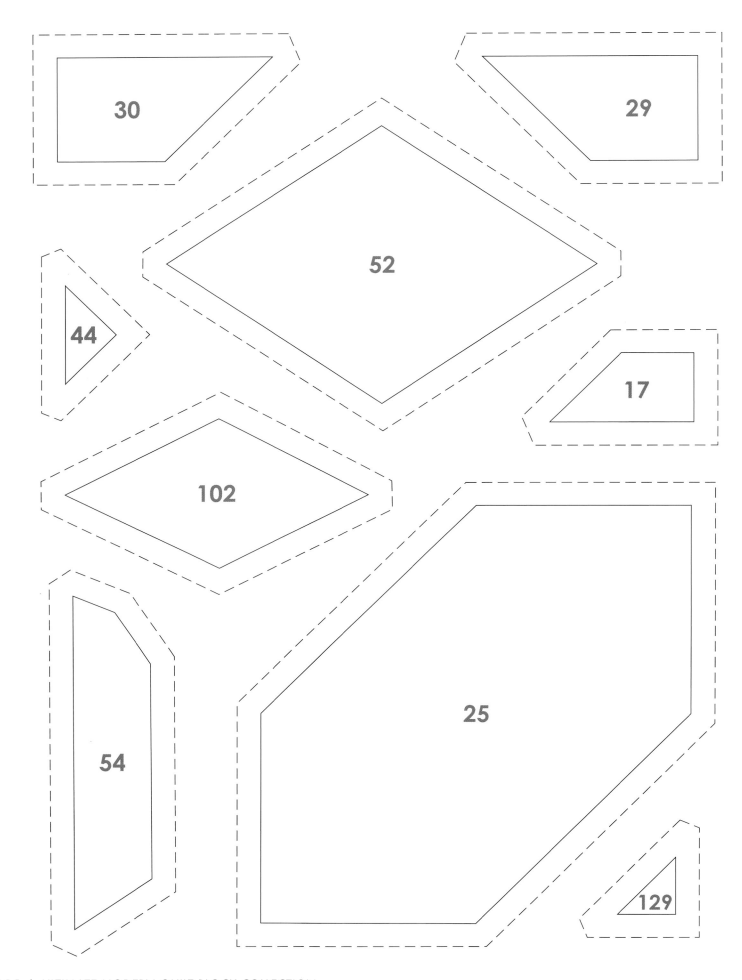

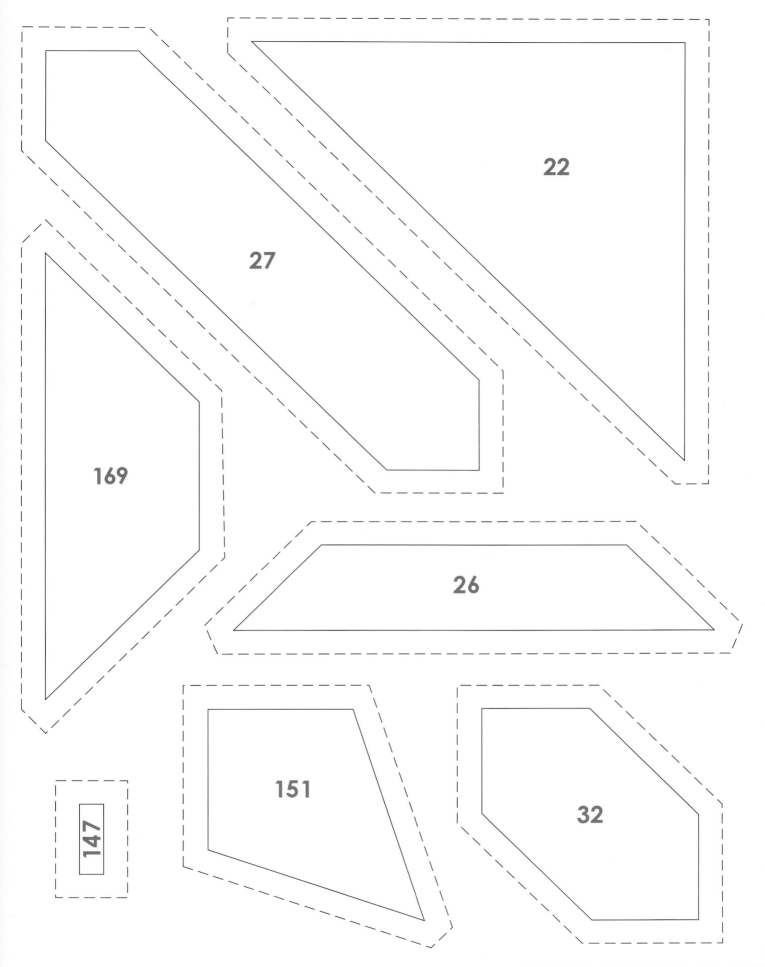

22

27

169

26

151

147

32

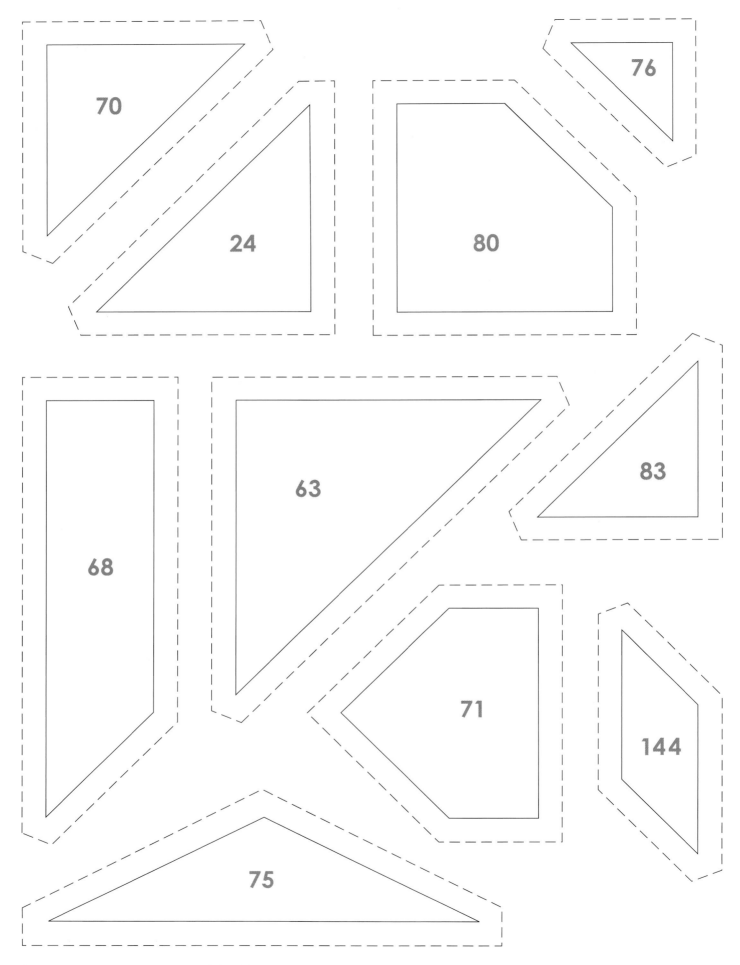

70

24

76

80

83

68

63

71

144

75

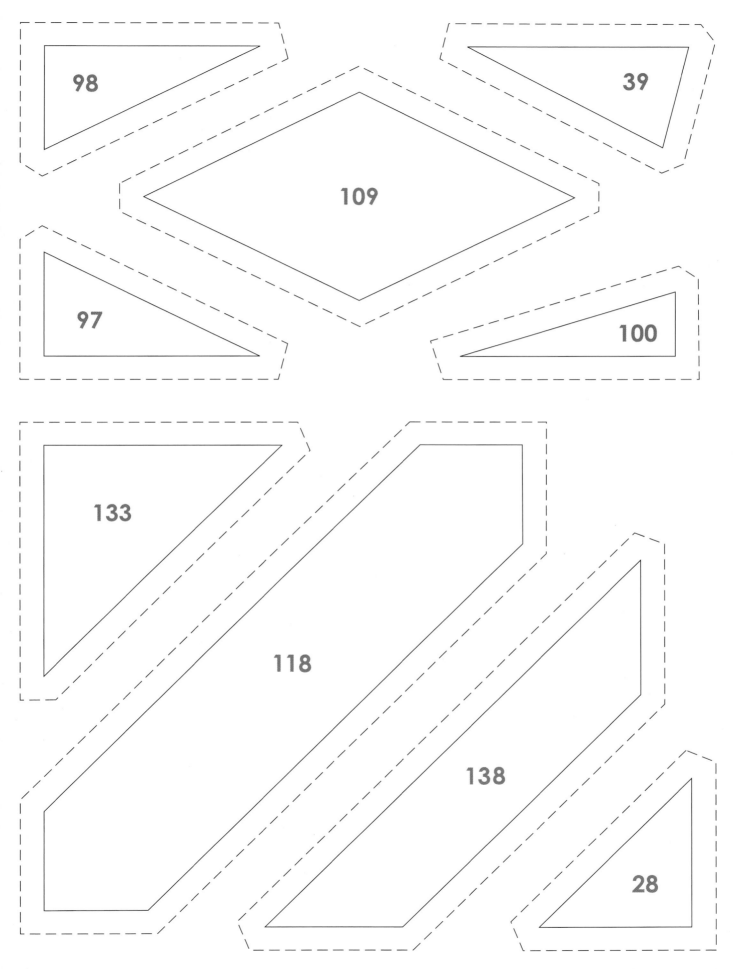

98

39

109

97

100

133

118

138

28

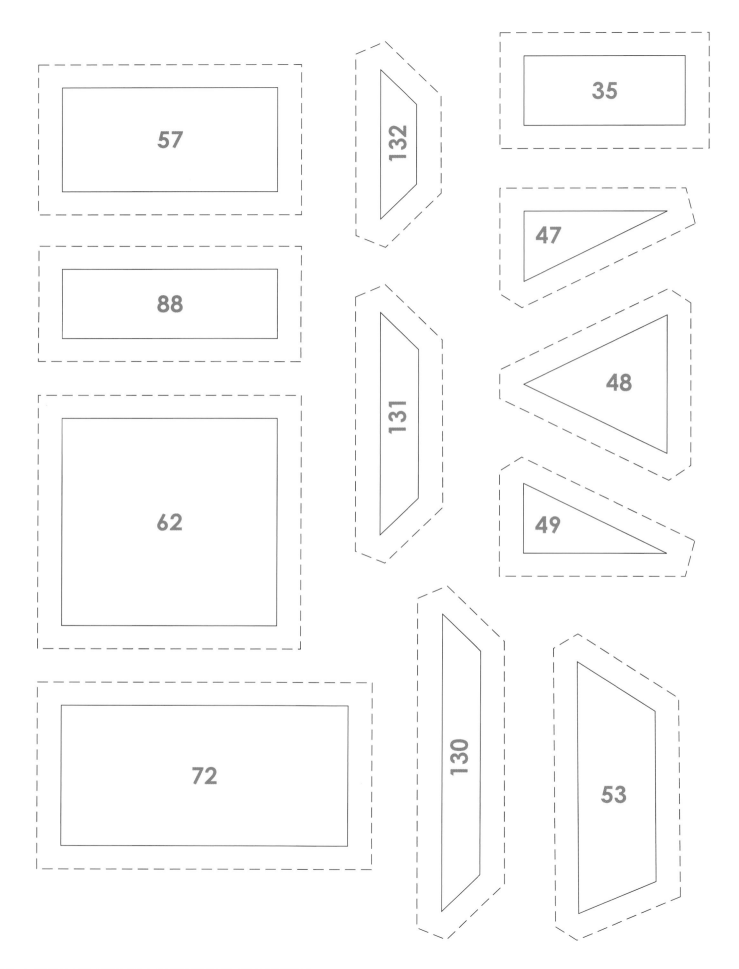

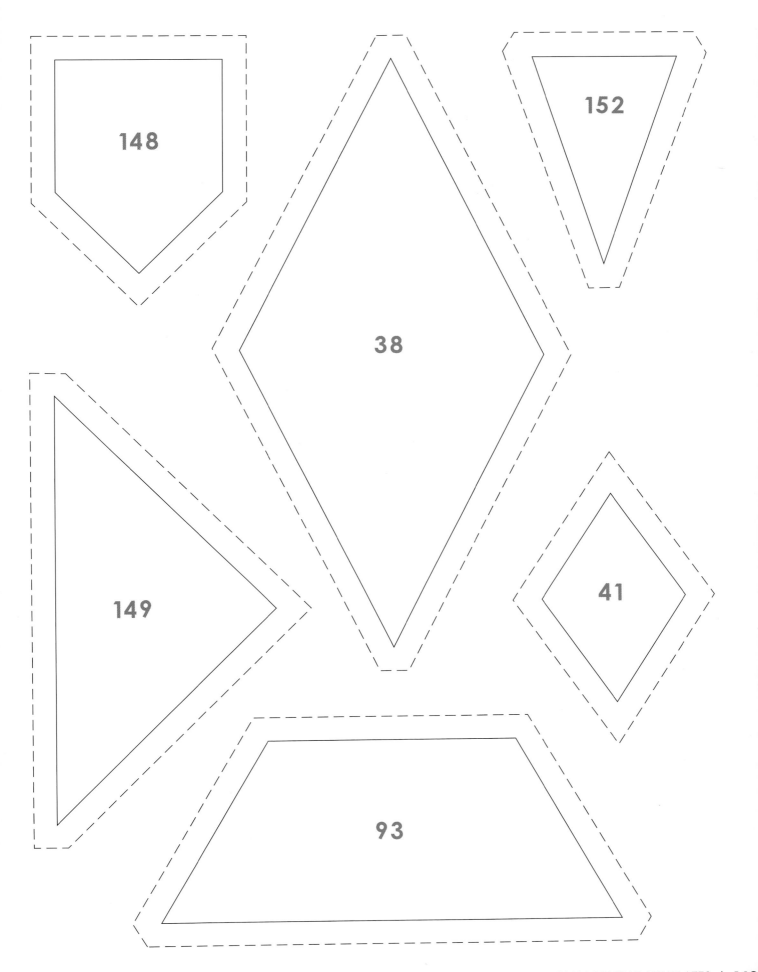

148

152

38

149

41

93

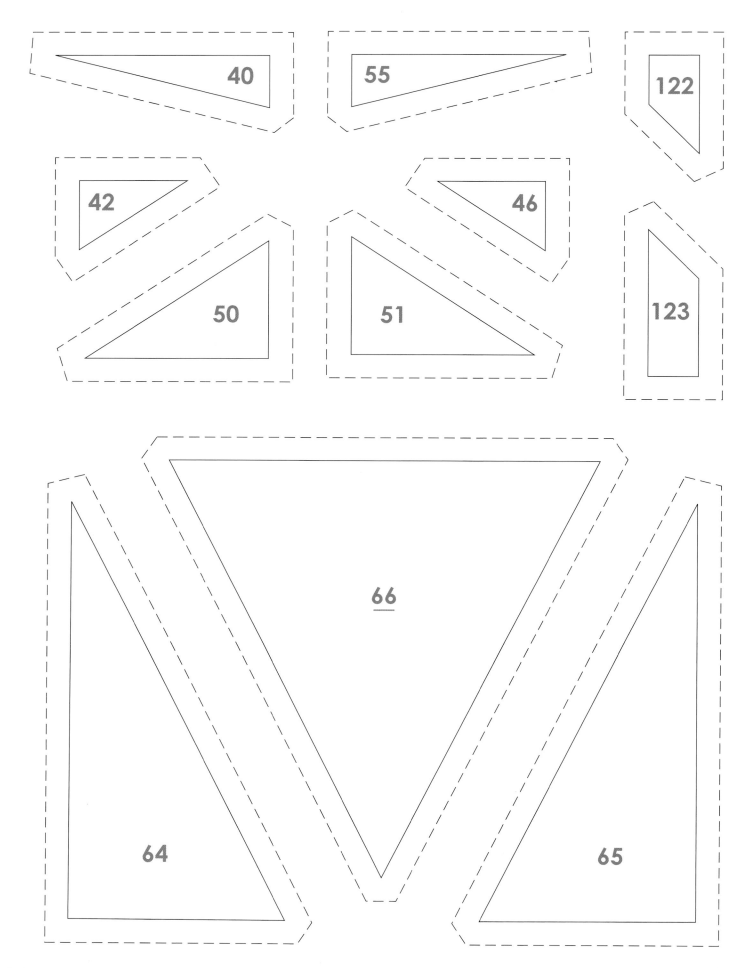

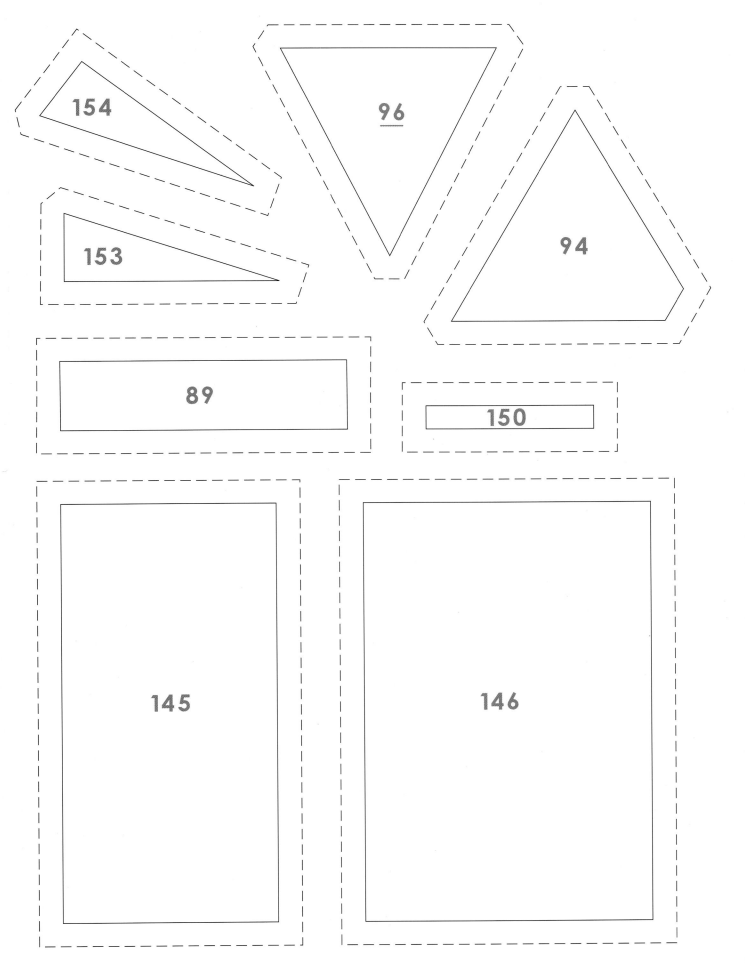

154

96

153

94

89

150

145

146

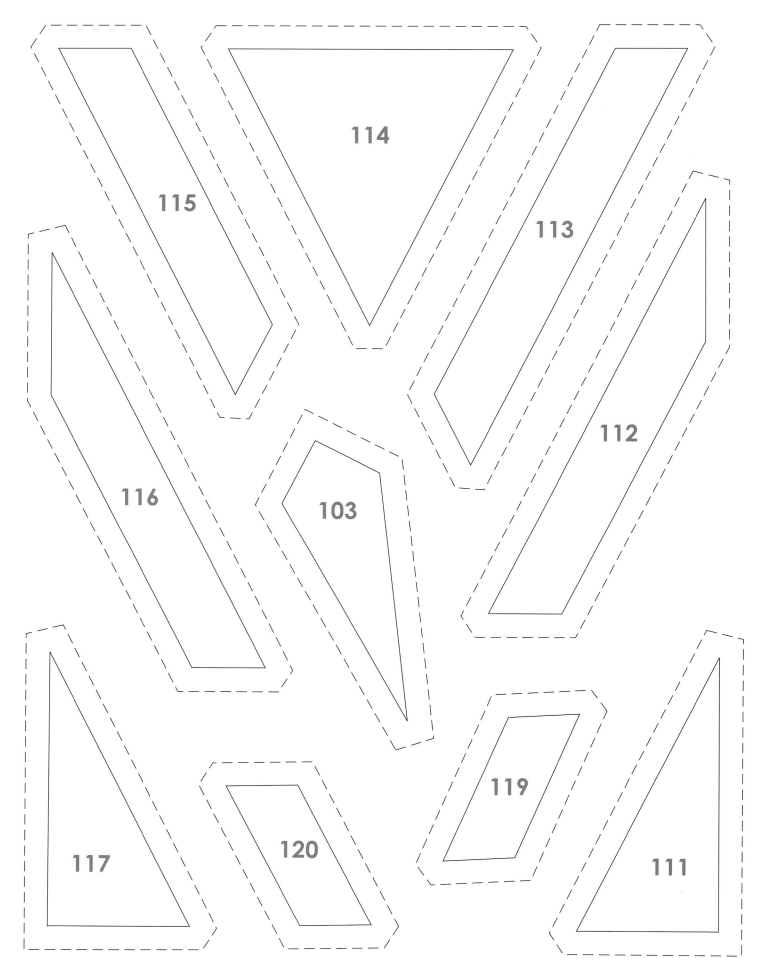

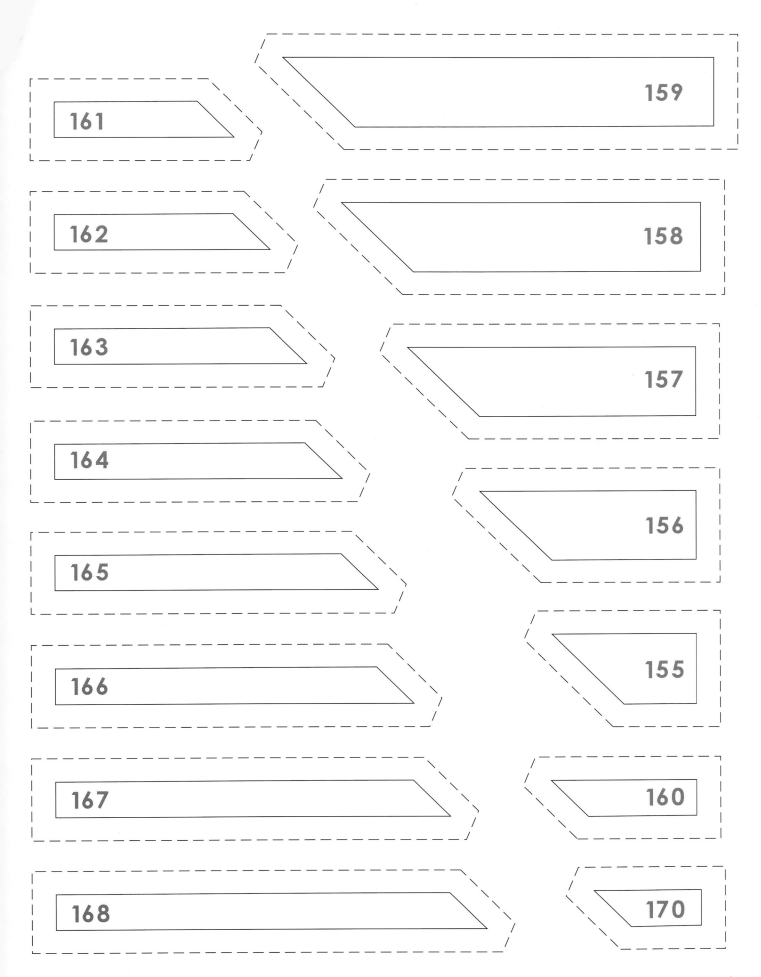

About the Author

Born and raised in Michigan, Daisy Dodge is a Midwestern girl at heart. Daisy graduated from the Columbus College of Art & Design in Columbus, Ohio, where she studied both commercial and fine art with a focus on advertising and printmaking. Her favorite medium was limestone lithography, which is where she fell in love with process-driven art mediums. This led her down many roads to exploring and honing skills in techniques like collaging, stained glass, and quilting.

Daisy's career in product design & development took her from Ohio to Michigan to Minnesota and landed her in New York, where she resided for over 20 years before moving to Florida in 2021.

Daisy has been quilting for over 30 years, making her first stitch in 1992. It all started when she and her mother signed up for an afternoon "Introduction to Quilting" class. Daisy never expected to fall in love with the art of quilting like she did. From that day forward, she was hooked and has been quilting (and collecting fabric) ever since. Daisy began designing her own quilting patterns early on, and has a natural knack for creative and interesting color and design combinations.

In addition to quilting, Daisy specializes in acrylic painting and collage art; she has won dozens of national awards for her work. You can view some of her portfolio at www.daisydodgeart.com.

Index

Template	Used in Block (by number)
1	11, 20, 30, 33, 108
2	11, 30, 33, 43, 45
3	11, 33, 34, 36, 56
4	6, 20, 29, 56, 108
5	4, 5, 12, 26, 27, 37, 40, 42, 46, 60, 64, 67, 71, 73, 82, 96, 105, 106
6	5, 67, 96, 106
7	67
8	67
9	7, 70, 87, 96, 102, 112
10	70, 87
11	70, 87
12	70, 87
13	70, 87
14	70, 87
15	70, 87
16	70, 87
17	7, 96
18	7, 96
19	7
20	7
21	7
22	7, 55, 87, 94, 112
23	94
24	13, 15, 18, 22, 36, 42, 44, 50, 57, 58, 61, 63, 86, 90, 94, 104, 113
25	22
26	18
27	18
28	12, 40, 64, 82, 110
29	12, 40, 110
30	12, 40, 110
31	12, 26, 37, 64, 71, 73, 82
32	60
33	50
34	50
35	50
36	31
37	31
38	31
39	17
40	17
41	49
42	49
43	1, 4, 10, 19, 30, 47, 49, 62, 80, 99
44	1, 4, 39, 47, 49, 75, 77, 79, 81, 88, 111
45	1, 4, 39, 47, 49, 77, 88
46	49
47	9, 29, 43, 85
48	9, 29, 43, 85
49	9, 29, 43, 85
50	78
51	78
52	78
53	78
54	78
55	17
56	19, 35, 75, 92, 95
57	3, 14, 52, 53, 65, 71, 109
58	61, 72
59	4
60	4, 65
61	3, 42, 53, 65, 71, 89, 109
62	34, 40, 56, 69, 90, 100, 104

Template	Used in Block (by number)
63	21, 58, 63, 74, 86
64	38, 97
65	38, 84, 97
66	97
67	109
68	16
69	16
70	14, 16, 76, 92
71	14
72	62, 98
73	2, 10, 20, 29, 51, 76, 80, 98, 108
74	35, 76, 92
75	28, 48
76	39, 75, 79, 81, 111
77	3
78	74
79	74
80	105
81	10, 45, 51, 59, 68, 80, 107
82	74
83	15, 44, 113
84	15, 44, 113
85	15, 44, 113
86	11, 20, 30, 33, 45, 51, 54, 59, 68, 69, 103, 107, 108
87	24
88	20, 32, 59, 68, 69
89	68, 80, 98
90	68
91	51
92	24
93	24
94	24
95	24
96	23, 32
97	23, 28, 32, 48
98	23, 28, 32, 48
99	35
100	66, 83
101	66, 83
102	66, 83
103	25
104	25
105	25
106	41
107	41
108	41
109	48
110	63
111	8
112	8
113	8
114	8
115	8
116	8
117	8
118	91
119	9
120	9
121	46
122	81
123	81
124	88
125	88

Template	Used in Block (by number)
126	88
127	88
128	88
129	72
130	72
131	72
132	72
133	91
134	45
135	45
136	45
137	45
138	91
139	45
140	45
141	45
142	45
143	45
144	46
145	93, 110
146	111
147	103
148	103
149	103
150	103
151	101
152	101
153	101
154	101
155	96, 102
156	96, 102
157	102
158	102
159	102
160	112
161	112
162	112
163	112
164	112
165	112
166	112
167	112
168	112
169	37
170	112

Blocks	Used in quilt(s)
1	Bauhaus
2	Bauhaus, Valentino Francine, Treasure Island
3	Bauhaus
4	Bauhaus
5	Bauhaus, Valentino Francine
6	Bauhaus, Valentino Francine, Treasure Island
7	Bauhaus
8	Bauhaus, Valentino Francine
9	Bauhaus
10	Bauhaus
11	Bauhaus, Treasure Island
12	Bauhaus
13	Bauhaus, Valentino Francine
14	Bauhaus
15	Bauhaus
16	Bauhaus
17	Bauhaus
18	Bauhaus
19	Bauhaus
20	Bauhaus, Valentino Francine
21	Bauhaus, Valentino Francine
22	Bauhaus
23	Bauhaus
24	Bauhaus, Valentino Francine, Treasure Island
25	Bauhaus, Valentino Francine
26	Bauhaus
27	Bauhaus, Treasure Island
28	Bauhaus
29	Bauhaus
30	Bauhaus, Valentino Francine
31	Bauhaus, Valentino Francine, Treasure Island
32	Bauhaus
33	Bauhaus, Valentino Francine, Treasure Island
34	Bauhaus, Valentino Francine
35	Bauhaus, Valentino Francine
36	Bauhaus, Valentino Francine
37	Bauhaus, Valentino Francine
38	Bauhaus
39	Bauhaus
40	Bauhaus
41	Bauhaus
42	Bauhaus, Valentino Francine, Treasure Island
43	Bauhaus
44	Bauhaus
45	Bauhaus, Valentino Francine, Treasure Island
46	Bauhaus
47	Bauhaus
48	Bauhaus
49	Bauhaus, Valentino Francine
50	Bauhaus, Valentino Francine
51	Bauhaus, Valentino Francine
52	Bauhaus
53	Bauhaus, Valentino Francine
54	Bauhaus, Racing Hearts, Valentino Francine
55	Bauhaus, Racing Hearts, Valentino Francine
56	Bauhaus

Blocks	Used in quilt(s)
57	Bauhaus, Valentino Francine
58	Bauhaus, Valentino Francine
59	Bauhaus
60	Bauhaus, Valentino Francine
61	Bauhaus, Valentino Francine
62	Bauhaus, Valentino Francine
63	Bauhaus, Valentino Francine
64	Bauhaus
65	Bauhaus, Valentino Francine
66	Bauhaus, Valentino Francine, Treasure Island
67	Bauhaus, Racing Hearts, Valentino Francine
68	Bauhaus, Valentino Francine
69	Bauhaus, Valentino Francine
70	Bauhaus
71	Bauhaus
72	Bauhaus
73	Bauhaus
74	Bauhaus, Valentino Francine
75	Bauhaus
76	Bauhaus, Valentino Francine
77	Bauhaus, Valentino Francine
78	Bauhaus
79	Bauhaus, Valentino Francine, Treasure Island
80	Bauhaus, Valentino Francine, Treasure Island
81	Bauhaus, Valentino Francine, Treasure Island
82	Bauhaus
83	Bauhaus, Valentino Francine, Treasure Island
84	Bauhaus
85	Bauhaus
86	Bauhaus, Treasure Island
87	Bauhaus, Racing Hearts, Treasure Island
88	Bauhaus, Valentino Francine
89	Bauhaus, Treasure Island
90	Bauhaus, Valentino Francine, Treasure Island
91	Bauhaus
92	Valentino Francine, Treasure Island
93	Valentino Francine
94	Valentino Francine
95	Valentino Francine
96	Valentino Francine
97	Valentino Francine, Treasure Island
98	Valentino Francine, Treasure Island
99	Valentino Francine
100	Valentino Francine
101	Valentino Francine
102	Treasure Island
103	Valentino Francine
104	
105	
106	
107	
108	
109	Treasure Island
110	
111	
112	Racing Hearts, Valentino Francine
113	Valentino Francine